nextstep

VOLUME 2

Discipleship is a series of next steps.

The Evangelical Catholic

the WORD
among us ®
Press

Published by The Word Among Us Press
7115 Guilford Drive, Suite 100
Frederick, Maryland 21704

24 23 22 21 20   1 2 3 4 5

ISBN: 978-1-59325-383-7
eISBN: 978-1-59325-384-4

Nihil Obstat: Msgr. Michael Morgan, J.D., J.C.L.
       Censor Librorum
       January 13, 2020

Imprimatur: +Most Rev. Felipe J. Estevez, S.T.D.
       Diocese of St. Augustine
       January 13, 2020

Library of Congress Control Number: 2019915077

Made and printed in the United States of America.

CONTENTS

Introduction

Let us throw off everything that hinders and the sin that
so easily entangles. And let us run with perseverance
the race marked out for us, fixing our eyes on Jesus,
the pioneer and perfecter of faith.
—Hebrews 12:1-2, NIV

In Part 1, we talked about "deification"—the idea that we can all be made more into Christ and become more God-like through grace. Baptism and conversion set us free from sin, so we can live freely the life God has made for us. Our first yes is to trust the God of these precious promises.

In Part 2, we considered the explicit call to discipleship—the idea that we need to make following Jesus the defining yes of our lives. Come what may, we are followers of Jesus Christ and his way! We commit to daily practices for the ongoing formation of our hearts and to develop the habits of discipleship.

In Part 3, we continue the journey of growing in discipleship, looking even more closely at the nature of freedom. Freedom is more than a one-time transaction by grace. Like any good parent, God wants us to grow in human and spiritual maturity as we acquire the tastes of God's kingdom: choosing for ourselves virtue over vice. This is the way of freedom. We do not merely sneak into God's kingdom by a grace-filled declaration that you and I are allowed entrance. We actually become fit for the kingdom itself, by living in it even now and acclimating to God's ways. Jesus came not only to forgive our sins but also to lead us into freedom and victory over "everything that hinders" (Hebrews 12:1, NIV).

In Part 4, we will begin to be equipped to help others take their next steps in following Jesus. As we grow to seek what Jesus seeks and love what Jesus loves, we will emanate more of Jesus' "flavor" into our world. Though there are many diverse ways to be the Lord's salt, light, and fragrance in the world, Part 4 focuses specifically on showing person-to-person love and care for the individuals the Lord has placed in our lives. We are each called to help a few others take their next steps on their way with Jesus.

Our journey of discipleship is never over. We can always grow closer to God. But the good news is that anyone on the road can help guide a fellow traveler.

An Acquired Taste

Andre

I love broccoli.

I really love brussels sprouts.

Don't get me wrong. I still love a good ole greasy McDonald's meal, but the enjoyment of French fries and broccoli are different experiences. A Micky D's binge can properly be described, for me, as a "guilty pleasure." Along with my temporary satiation comes that nagging awareness that I've just filled my body with a substance that only detracts from its health and longevity. If I manage to forget this fact, my body reminds me with rumblings and aches within the hour.

Not so with vegetables. While it may be (much) less exciting or addictive, the experience of enjoying healthy food is another level of "good"—one which most parents hope their children will experience for themselves. It's different from French fries and candy. There's no downside. It contributes to everything good for our brains and bodies. And to the one who has acquired the taste for vegetables, eating them is delightful.

Some things in God's kingdom—like justice, meekness, humility, generosity and self-control—can be acquired tastes. In our immaturity, even though we may be "saved by grace" and forgiven, we still prefer the "taste" of many vices over that of virtue. Our concupiscence remains. At times, we manage to fight back against our urges to sin, and at other times, we dive in with guilty pleasure and then run back to the Lord in repentance. In his love and mercy, he never tires of lifting us up—thanks be to God! But let us never think that this situation describes the fullness of life and freedom in Christ! No! God gave us spiritual taste buds, so to speak, that can mature with repeated exposure to virtue and all that is good. We may have to choke down some vegetables we don't like much at first—things like faithfulness to prayer or giving money away or trying to bear wrongs patiently or sharing a faith story with someone else. But before we know it, we find ourselves enjoying the taste of these kingdom ways more and more. They're so deeply good for us—and for those around us!

By grace, with effort, and through many failures, we can actually get somewhere in victory over sin and vice! We can experience not merely a white-knuckled, last-minute victory of self-control over the pull of pornography or gluttony or ranting in anger, but *distaste* for these very things, such that leaving them behind becomes . . . dare we say . . . easy! This is true freedom: not merely to hold our noses and force down God's laws but to *relish their sweetness*.

Do not be discouraged if your taste buds are not yet fully attuned to all that is good, true, and beautiful. None of us are there yet. But this is the road of transformation upon which we all must travel as Jesus' followers. Jesus called it the narrow way (see Matthew 7:13-14), and it leads to "the glorious freedom of the children of God" (Romans 8:21, NABRE). Our ongoing transformation consists in acquiring God's own tastes. As we grow "in union with Jesus, we seek what he seeks and we love what he loves" (Pope Francis, *Evangelii Gaudium*, 267).

Not only do we grow to acquire the tastes of Jesus and his kingdom, but in doing so, we also become "salt of the earth" (Matthew 5:13) or what St. Paul called "the aroma of Christ" (2 Corinthians 2:15). With the help of our witness and actions, others too can better acquire the tastes of God's kingdom.

This volume of *Nextstep* presents various reflections and practices to help us continue on the narrow path and further develop our tastes for God's ways.

PART 3

HIT YOUR STRIDE: MATURING AS A DISCIPLE

1

Virtue and Vice

In roaring winds and crashing seas,
an anchor holds the vessel fast.
Hope anchors us.

Faithful in Small Matters: Human Virtues in Increments

Think about a goal you have struggled with, strived for, fought for, or sacrificed for. Perhaps you were the kid who ended up as an all-state athlete, or maybe you practiced daily to become first chair violinist in the orchestra. Perhaps you participated in an advanced training so you could lead coworkers on a project. Or maybe you know the blood, sweat, and tears involved in rearing a child with special needs or caring for a parent with dementia.

Regardless of the specific skill, your abilities in this area didn't appear overnight. They required both time and effort. You didn't become a master of addressing the challenges of autism, swimming one hundred meters at top speed, or fixing diesel engines just by *wanting* the skills necessary. You fought for those skills, and that fight spanned years.

Beyond this prolonged effort, with skills growing slowly and in increments, we know that the abilities of an Olympic athlete and the skills of a welder or a nurse all represent value. While the Olympic athlete may appear on television and receive a medal, that athlete is certainly not more valuable to the world than the welder or the nurse. The world's division of skills into "small" or "large" does not reflect the worth of a skill. All skills involve sacrifice.

St. Francis de Sales spoke on these issues in his *Introduction to the Devout Life*. To serve God "as he wishes we must have great care to serve him well both in great, lofty matters and in small, unimportant things. With love we can capture his heart by the one just as well as by the other."[1]

If God doesn't call us to make the "great sacrifices," de Sales explained, we can grow in virtue in the small things by bearing "patiently the slight injuries, the little inconveniences, the inconsequential losses" that come to us daily.[2]

As De Sales reminded us, "Great opportunities to serve God rarely present themselves but little ones are frequent."[3] We should take advantage of every one of these little opportunities to grow and to please him.

Growing toward the Ultimate Goal

Obedience helps us move toward sanctification. This faithfulness in small matters trains our spiritual muscles, or we could say that it develops our spiritual taste buds. This commitment to obedience to Christ transforms us. Merely refraining from sin does not lead us to grow into the fullness of our true nature. Remember the discussion of Mr. Nice Guy in Part 1? Mr. Nice Guy is not enough.

We need to *grow in virtue*. And we need to grow this way intentionally and with specificity.

From a psychological perspective, it makes sense. Elite athletes using sports psychology to reach excellence know that a positive statement carries far more efficacy than a negative one. Olympic coaches will tell you the power of positive "self-talk."

Try this exercise:

"Don't think about purple poodles."

What did you think about?

Yep, you probably thought about those poodles. A better way to get someone to move away from purple poodles is to give them a positive alternative.

"Think about yellow elephants."

You probably didn't think about purple poodles!

In obedience and sanctification, we can focus on *virtues* to grow. With "our eyes fixed on Jesus, the leader and perfecter of faith" (Hebrews 12:2, NABRE), no longer will we simply avoid sin. We can grow in holiness by cultivating virtue.

The three theological virtues are:

1. Faith
2. Hope
3. Charity

As with the seven deadly sins we discussed in Part 1, there are also three theological virtues and four cardinal virtues to make seven essential virtues to pursue. The four cardinal virtues are:

1. Prudence
2. Justice
3. Fortitude
4. Temperance

With our Baptism and these virtues, we become receptive to seven special gifts of the Holy Spirit, namely:

1. Understanding
2. Knowledge
3. Wisdom
4. Fear of the Lord
5. Counsel
6. Piety
7. Fortitude

The *Catechism of the Catholic Church* urges us to remember that the human virtues have their roots "in the theological virtues, which adapt man's faculties for participation in the divine nature" (1812).

Hope: Our Anchor

Clare

Having lived on two sailboats, I can tell you how marvelous an anchor is. Such a small tool to do such an enormous task! Anchors don't simply hold a boat in place. They secure a boat to keep her from foundering on rocks, on treacherous lee shores (downwind places), in roaring winds and in crashing seas. They hold the vessel fast.

Hope anchors us. In Christian tradition, an anchor symbolizes hope:

> So when God desired to show more convincingly to the heirs of the promise the unchangeable character of his purpose, he interposed with an oath, so that through two unchangeable things, in which it is impossible that God should prove false, we who have fled for refuge might have strong encouragement to seize the hope set before us. We have this as a sure and steadfast anchor of the soul, a hope that enters into the inner shrine behind the curtain, where Jesus has gone as a forerunner on our behalf, having become a high priest for ever after the order of Melchizedek. (Hebrews 6:17-20)

Hope is the theological virtue by which we desire the kingdom of heaven and eternal life as our happiness, placing our trust in Christ's promises and relying not on our own strength, but on the help of the grace of the Holy Spirit. "Let us hold fast the confession of our hope without wavering, for he who promised is faithful." "The Holy Spirit . . . he poured out upon us richly through Jesus Christ our Savior, so that we might be justified by his grace and become heirs in hope of eternal life." (*Catechism*, 1817)

While bleak times can demoralize us, we must call on God to fill us with the hope that keeps us ever mindful of his grace and protection. This hope cultivates in us magnanimity (a confidence to do great things in God) and humility (a recognition that one's gifts come from God). We sin against hope when we presume (take for granted God's goodness or believe we can succeed without God) or despair (give up on God's grace).

In All Things Hope

Yes, I have spoken, I will accomplish it;
   I have planned it, and I will do it.
Listen to me, you fainthearted,
   far from the victory of justice:
I am bringing on that victory, it is not far off,
   my salvation shall not tarry.
—Isaiah 46:11-13, NABRE

Andrea

God's time.
God's promises.
God's faithfulness.
God's ability.

My doubt.

"Fainthearted." The word describes me. My heart lacks the needed strength. My love lacks the needed courage. My heart faints, flounders. It surrenders to worries and anxieties instead of to the surpassing strength of God.

You who seem far off but are not. "It is not far off, my salvation shall not tarry" (Isaiah 46:13). So often I have experienced this: lack of hope, lack of faith that God will come through, that whatever seemingly unbearable situation I'm facing will end. Then suddenly, I meet *restoration*. Only in retrospect do I recognize that this relief hid just around the corner, that salvation was almost there.

During a struggle, I've sometimes tasted the grace of hope: *This will not last forever. The Lord has an end to this suffering in store. His salvation is near. God is able. He keeps his promises.*

Those days are gifts, and they keep me moving forward. On other days, I've heard instead the nagging voice of the deceiver: *God has abandoned you to this fate. There is no end. God might be able, but he's not willing to save you. You're never going to feel whole.*

Those thoughts don't strengthen me. They give instead a *false* sense of strength; they give *calluses*. These calluses ready me for more days of disappointment, more seemingly fruitless novenas, more deep-down aching. They also close me off and construct walls between me and God.

Hope is so, so hard. It requires vulnerability. It doesn't involve protective calluses. It requires us to *feel*. Feel the pain, feel the disappointment, feel the longing. Feeling means keeping our hearts open to God. *"How long, Lᴏʀᴅ?"* (Psalm 13:2, NABRE). We make the ancient cry. Our hearts must *ache* instead of hardening.

Hope allows the pain; hope accepts the suffering. Hope cries out, submits itself to scourges, undergoes the beatings, and bears the shame. Hope keeps walking, stumbling forward.

You who seem "far from the victory of justice. . . . it is not far off, my salvation shall not tarry (Isaiah 46:12, 13).

Hope is the virtue of the cross, the grace of Calvary. Mary and John look at the cross; Jesus suffers the cross—*You who seem "far from the victory of justice"*—they hope the truth: God is able. God's salvation will not tarry.

Hope waits through the night of Good Friday into the dawn of Easter. It persists through Holy Saturday, looking at death, at a tomb closed tight, still expecting the God of the impossible to bring forth life.

Hope remains faithful in all things.

What Would You Give for Your Life?

Jesus "came that they may have life, and have it abundantly" (John 10:10). He goes on to say, "I am the good shepherd. The good shepherd lays down his life for the sheep" (10:11).

Our lives are precious to us, as they should be. We don't like to think about their fragility and their briefness. But if there's one thing we can all say for sure, it's that someday we will die. But here's the thing: that's why Jesus is such *good* news! He offers to save us, if we'll let him.

> Then Jesus told his disciples, "If any man would come after me, let him deny himself and take up his cross and follow me.

For whoever would save his life will lose it, and whoever loses his life for my sake will find it. For what will it profit a man, if he gains the whole world and forfeits his life? Or what shall a man give in return for his life?" (Matthew 16:24-26)

What is more important than your life? If you put things into proper perspective, probably only the most beloved relatives or causes seem worth dying for. And yet most of us hand over our lives to foods, money, status, habits, and even addictions that slowly kill us. Even worse, we allow sin to creep in and tear us apart from the inside out. Self-denial is hard, and carrying the cross is hard. Following Jesus isn't easy. But is it worth it? What use is it to have the whole world but not your life?

Jesus makes good on his word. He is willing, and in fact does lay down his life in order to save us from death. The question is: are you willing to lay down your own life in order to save it?

Fully Alive

Andrea

My husband tells me that when he hikes and reaches the pinnacle of a mountain, he feels *more alive*. I know what he means, and yet, I can't help but think, isn't life sort of a binary thing? Like either you're breathing or you're not? Yet I too can point to times in my life when I felt like the walking dead, still breathing in and out, but listless and without direction. Maybe it's not so straightforward.

We recently considered Jesus' promise that "whoever loses his life for my sake will find it" (Matthew 16:25). Was Jesus asking people to literally sacrifice their lives for his sake? Many martyrs have done just that. But "losing your life" for Christ's sake has an additional definition. When St. Paul tells the Romans, "We were buried therefore with [Jesus] by baptism into death, so that as Christ was raised from the dead by the glory of the Father, we too might walk in newness of life" (Romans 6:4), he's not only talking about the resurrection. The "death" to the old life and walking in a "newness of life" are not only for after you stop breathing. You can have this newness *now*.

We hope you've never been part of an argument in which one party used the strong words "You're dead to me!" The phrase suggests that, for the speaker, the hearer no longer exists, no longer matters, and is completely cut off. When we follow Jesus—when we agree to take up our crosses and follow him and when we say we're all in—we say to our selfishness and to our sin, "You're dead to me!"

> The death [Jesus] died he died to sin, once for all, but the life he lives he lives to God. So you also must consider yourselves dead to sin and alive to God in Christ Jesus. (Romans 6:10-11)

When we're dead to sin, it no longer exists to us, it no longer has power over us, and we have completely cut ourselves off from it. Instead, everything we are and all that we have are oriented to God. We live only for God and for nothing else.

Action Step: The Particular Examination

> Therefore, since we are surrounded by so great a cloud of witnesses, let us also lay aside every weight, and sin which clings so closely, and let us run with perseverance the race that is set before us, looking to Jesus the pioneer and perfecter of our faith, who for the joy that was set before him endured the cross, despising the shame, and is seated at the right hand of the throne of God.
>
> Consider him who endured from sinners such hostility against himself, so that you may not grow weary or fainthearted. In your struggle against sin you have not yet resisted to the point of shedding your blood. (Hebrews 12:1-4)

Sin weighs us down; it entangles us. We can't run fast after Jesus when we're bound up by sin.

In past sections, we've discussed examining our consciences and our actions and preparing for Confession. Let's add to these practices the *particular examination*.

You may feel like you're always on the defensive when it comes to sin: trying to avoid it, warding it off, resisting temptation. A particular examination lets you take the offensive against a particular sin by preemptively asking for grace and for virtues that combat the sin you struggle with.

Choose one sin you want to avoid and/or a corresponding virtue to foster.

Every evening for two weeks or more, take one to two minutes to review your day:

- Did you avoid this sin/exercise this virtue?

- If you failed, ask for forgiveness. If you succeeded, give praise and gratitude.

- Pray for the grace to resist this sin/exercise this virtue tomorrow.

2

Maturing in Prayer

Nothing—not our distractions,
not our weaknesses, and not the end of the
world—is reason enough to not pray.

Prayer Life

"Prayer life" and "life of prayer": both suggest that prayer is
more than an activity; somehow it's a "life" or lifestyle. In this
section, we will continue our journey into a deeper life of prayer,
building on the habits and practices we explored in Part 2.

Andrea

Two months before my wedding, I had a realization. I'd
had no experience of *forever*. Twenty-four years of life
had passed in chunks predetermined by school boards:
five before school, five elementary, four middle, four high,
four college, two internship. Now, preparing to promise "I

will love you and honor you all the days of my life" made me consider *forever*. Marriage wasn't another chunk. It required all of me for all the days of my life.

Prayer is a relationship with Jesus not unlike a marriage. It requires all of me for all the days of my life.

Prayer follows the contours of a life. There are joyful periods and dull ones, times of growth and of stagnation. But as a relationship, as a commitment, it is a *forever* experience.

In a mature life of prayer, God gets everything. When we hit rough patches, we bring them to Jesus. When we mourn and are angry and wonder why things happened the way they did, we bring that grief and those frustrations to Jesus in all their rawness. When things fall into place and life is better than we ever dreamed, we bring our wonder and happiness to Jesus too. God gets all of it. Let Jesus have all of you for all the days of your life.

That's a life of prayer.

A Promise to Persist

Andrea

I fell in love with Jesus when I was nineteen years old. Kneeling before the raised Eucharist in the midst of my fellow students, I felt for the first time a joy that welled up within me and made my toes tap. Jesus was my beloved, the joy of my heart. My soul soared.

That spring, prayer was sweet. Every evening, I closed the door to my room, shut out my roommates, and sat up in bed, propping open my Bible on my knees. I read. I felt God's unique concern for me as, night after night, I prayed through the Book of Psalms. Every psalm seemed chosen for me. The Holy Spirit spoke through the words and spoke straight to my heart.

I remember moments from my prayer during this season the way I remember those sweet first moments of meeting and dating my husband—moments characterized by beauty and love and importance that are marked firmly in my memory.

These days didn't last forever, and perhaps that's why they stay with me. The quickness and intensity of love's first expression lengthened and deepened into something strong enough to persist through difficulty, disinterest, and distraction.

The promise of prayer is life. It beckons us into the life of God and, in so doing, recreates us as those followers of Christ who desire to live with him forever. "To whom shall we go? You have the words of eternal life" (John 6:68) becomes our refrain even in times of hardship, while "How great thou art!" bursts from us when we touch God's goodness once again.

Prayer requires a commitment, a promise to persist come what may. According to St. Teresa of Avila (a sixteenth-century Carmelite mystic and Doctor of the Church), all those who begin along the road of prayer "must have a great and very resolute determination to persevere until reaching the end, come what may, happen what may, whatever work is involved, whatever criticism arises, whether they arrive or whether they die on the road, or even if they don't have courage for the trials that are met, or if the whole world collapses."[4]

Nothing—not our distractions, not our weaknesses, not the end of the world—is reason enough to not pray. Why? Because prayer is how we open ourselves wider and wider to God. Prayer prepares our souls for the fullness of God we hope to know in heaven. Prayer is our only hope of getting there.

- **How has prayer changed for you over the course of your life in Christ? What seasons have you experienced?**

- **Describe the current season of your prayer life. What do you need right now to persist in prayer?**

No Need to Strive in Prayer

Do you hear it too? The voice that urges you to do it all, all the time? To be everything to everyone? Good isn't good enough. You feel the push to be the best father/mother, husband/wife, employee, student, friend . . . the list goes on.

While we must learn to persist in prayer, come what may, we must also avoid the opposite error of striving to make prayer everything *we* think it should be. Or to make ourselves everything *we* think we should be.

We work tirelessly to create a perfectly curated image for the world, but for what end?

In our striving to be accepted, we avoid the pain of rejection at all costs. Rejection by our trade, our community, our family, and our friends haunts us, but even more, we must convince *ourselves* that we are enough.

Henri Nouwen writes in *You Are the Beloved: Daily Meditations for Spiritual Living*, "Self-rejection is the greatest enemy of the spiritual life because it contradicts the sacred voice that calls us the beloved."[5]

Do you struggle with thinking and hoping that the next promotion, the perfect relationship, the vacation, the house, or the *thing* will be "it"? This pursuit keeps us preoccupied and driven while simultaneously bullying us into feeling like it's never enough.

No matter how hard or fast we run in this life, we cannot *earn* God's love.

So hear the words of your heavenly Father proclaimed over you today: "Behold, my servant whom I have chosen / my beloved with whom my soul is well pleased" (Matthew 12:18).

Let the words of your loving Father wash over the lies of inadequacy that try to steal your joy. Let God's love free you from the prison of striving.

Let your prayer life emerge as a response to this fundamental *given*: You are chosen and loved for all that you are, and all that you are not. You are his beloved.

As we set out to grow in prayer through challenges and temptations to give it up, let us first recall this foundational truth of our lives in Christ: God loves us.

Maturing in Prayer Is about Presence

What makes a disciple?

Jesus chose the twelve apostles for three reasons, according to Mark's Gospel: "to be with him," "to preach," and "to cast out demons" (3:14, 15). In Matthew's Gospel, prophesying and casting out demons do not, in and of themselves, constitute discipleship; they do not make a person fit for the kingdom of heaven (see 7:21-23). Both Gospels agree that Jesus chose twelve to be *with* him and to *know* him. It follows that those who are prepared to enter the kingdom of heaven are those who know and do the will of the Father.

Sticking with Jesus in the face of hardship, distraction, shame, our own sinfulness, or just plain boredom is not easy. Almost all of the Twelve whom Jesus chose to be with him ran from him in the face of persecution. Peter's first response to Jesus' power is to declare, "Depart from me, for I am a sinful man, O Lord" (Luke 5:8). And it seems that Peter, James, and John frequently fell asleep when Jesus asked them to go pray with him (see Mark 14:32-42; Luke 9:32).

In spite of his disciples' inconstancy, Jesus calls them to follow him. When Peter admits his sinfulness to Jesus while on the Lake of Gennesaret, Jesus doesn't disagree. And yet his response to Peter is not one of rebuke. Instead, he gives Peter the fisherman a new identity: "'Do not be afraid; henceforth you will be catching men.' And when they had brought their boats to land, they left everything and followed him" (Luke 5:10-11).

- **What are the greatest difficulties you currently face in prayer?**

- Rather than merely trying to overcome these (a worthy aim), can you also listen for Jesus' voice to you, loving you in the midst of your imperfect prayer life? What is he saying?

Taking Away the Candy

Andre

I hope that one day (not too soon) I receive the grace of getting to be a grandpa. I look forward to getting to play the "card" that grandparents get to play when spending time with grandkids—a card that parents shouldn't play as frequently. I call it "the candy card."

"It's so good to see you! Oh, and look, I brought you some treats!"

"Why don't we plan a weekend together? You can pick out your favorite meals and desserts!"

Grandparents deserve this luxury, you know—they've parented the hard way all those years! And now, in their older age, they get to play the candy card, doggone it! Why not make their interactions with their newest little loved ones all the more anticipated? Go for it, Gran and Gramps!

But we all know too much playing of the candy card, by parents or grandparents, stunts the growth and maturity of the children and the relationship. Kids can "get a bad case of the gimmies!" (At least that's what Mama and Papa Bear from the *Berenstain Bears* call it.)

What about with God?

Saints and spiritual writers have, for centuries, called the good feelings that often accompany prayer and discipleship "consolations." They are a *great* gift indeed. They help draw us to follow Christ. They can sweeten our relationship with the Lord and heighten our anticipation to spend time alone with him. God is the great giver who loves giving good gifts to his children, including spiritual consolations!

But as a loving Father, God also wants us to mature in loving him and loving others. He doesn't want us to turn to prayer only because it makes us feel good. Sometimes, God takes away the "candy." In certain seasons, God seems to withhold certain spiritual consolations that used to accompany our acts of devotion, our service, and our obedience. Dryness, boredom, doubt, restlessness, desolations, and many other struggles are part of our lives as Christians, and Jesus does not always wish to rush in and make us feel better with immediate consolations. He wants a growing, mature love in us that mirrors more and more his own selfless, fully-committed, and "all-in" love for us, which never faltered even in his darkest hours.

What a gracious and loving God we have! His promises to be with us and to strengthen us remain, despite whatever we may or may not *feel* in a given moment.

- **In what seasons of your life have you experienced deep spiritual consolation in the practices of discipleship?**

- **In what ways has God taken away some "candy" from you in order to refine your love for him, who alone can truly satisfy the deepest desires of your heart?**

Action Step: Make a Plan to Persist in Daily Prayer

Each of us encounters various challenges in prayer. In some ways, we always remain *beginners* as we stand before the Lord God of Hosts, seeking his face.

Yet we also learn many lessons over the course of a life of prayer; we can progress, we can grow, and we can overcome some difficulties—by grace and with our cooperation with grace.

The key lies in *showing up* for prayer, and this can be one of the hardest things to do!

The rest of this chapter contains tips and suggestions for building a daily habit of prayer in the face of common difficulties.

Schedule Time

Aim to spend at least fifteen minutes each day (1 percent of your day) with God in one uninterrupted period, not while driving or doing other activities. Don't multitask! Recall how you feel when you're in the middle of a conversation with a friend who suddenly brings out a smartphone and begins texting. It's a good habit to keep God's presence throughout the day when you're doing other things, but this prayer time is focused solely on God.

A scheduled time helps build the habit of prayer. Setting a regular time each day is the surest way to make your prayer time happen.

Pray in the Morning if Possible

Morning by morning he wakens, / . . . my ear / to hear.
—Isaiah 50:4

Praying and listening to God first thing in the morning is best for many people because nothing interferes with your prayer if nothing else is happening.

Morning prayer allows you to quite literally "seek *first* his kingdom" (Matthew 6:33, emphasis added). It also allows you the chance to make up your prayer at some later time in the day if an unforeseen circumstance interrupts your morning prayer time.

Praying first thing in the morning has been the preferred practice of many saints and Christians throughout history, and Jesus himself often rose before dawn to pray in solitude.

But pray how and when you can! It's more important to schedule a time each day than to schedule an ideal time you won't keep. If you cannot do your daily prayer time in the morning, we still recommend starting your day with a simple morning offering.

Don't Let the "Method" Get in the Way

The four steps of *lectio divina* can help, but don't let them limit you. Teresa of Avila called prayer "an intimate sharing between friends."[6] A conversation between friends would be strange and forced if it always followed a routine or formula. Try different ways to *talk*, *listen to*, and simply *be* with God.

Explore other prompts or methods for prayer. For example, use the Our Father or the Order of the Mass as an outline of the various types of prayers and petitions.

We've talked about this approach before, but you can use the first three things many children learn to say as an outline for prayer time: **Thank you, I'm Sorry,** and **Please.** It's as simple as that!

"Stop, look, and listen" is what you do at a railroad crossing. Prayer is like a railroad crossing. God is like a great train crossing the tracks of your life. You *want* to get run over by this train! So here is how you put yourself on the tracks in front of God.[7]

Sometimes words get in the way of deeper communication. Lovers stare into one another's eyes . . . wordlessly. Parents and children cuddle and say nothing. The only way to hear anyone, including God, is to be silent. Any friendship in which you are never quiet and attentive will eventually dissolve. We keep coming back to this: The Lord says, "Be still, and know that I am God" (Psalm 46:10). Begin and end each prayer time with a minute of silence to rest in God's presence.

Keep it real! Be yourself and come to God just as you are, not how you think you *should* be.

Set Achievable Goals

If fifteen minutes (1 percent of your day) is too difficult at first, start with a more achievable goal and work up from there.

If you're already faithful to 1 percent, consider working up to 2 percent or more! Offer the additional time for others or for some special intention.

If you miss a day, don't get discouraged; just get back on track. Try especially hard not to miss two days in a row.

Remember to try it for thirty days first. Use the thirty Scripture verses in The Evangelical Catholic's 1% Challenge™ (www.evangelicalcatholic.org/onepercent).

Use Helpful Resources, but Don't Let Them Distract You

There are many good books and Bible tools out there to help you read and apply God's word. But don't become a "commentary junky," or you may tend to put off praying for more learning. Communicating with God requires your heart to open, not your mind to fill. Simple, brief use of a few good resources can be a wonderful aid to praying with the Bible.

If you feel called to dig into more serious or academic study of the Bible (a recommended joy for those who love learning about God!), build in additional time for the disciplines of study and spiritual reading. Protect your fifteen minutes a day for direct dialogue with God through prayer and *lectio divina*.

Find more resources at www.evangelicalcatholic.org/resources-on-prayer-scripture.

Stay Motivated

Notice the fruits on days you pray. You'll see the fruits, and this experience will motivate you to pray every day.

Keep a notebook with brief insights, prayers, and Scripture passages that speak to you. Review weekly or at whatever frequency works best for you.

Occasionally read a short book on prayer. We recommend:

- Peter Kreeft, *Prayer for Beginners* (San Francisco, CA: Ignatius Press, 2000)
- Fr. Jacques Philippe, *Time for God*, trans. Helena Scott (New York, NY: Scepter Publishers, 1992)

Don't "Go It Alone"

Iron sharpens iron, / and one man sharpens another.
—Proverbs 27:17

If you *really* want to grow, ask a friend to commit to getting together regularly with you to explicitly discuss your prayer lives and what the Lord is doing in both of you. Share your experiences, goals, joys, and struggles. Pray for and with one another.

You may wish to seek out a good spiritual director.

Additional Tips

Don't overlook the human mechanisms that will enable you to be faithful to daily prayer: put it on your calendar, set the coffee maker the night before so that it's ready for your morning coffee date with Jesus, and make a commitment to ignore social media and email until you've prayed. Put your alarm on the other side of the room so that you don't waste fifteen minutes hitting the snooze bar!

If you are distracted, simply persevere. Take those distractions to prayer or write them down so that you can return to them at a better time. Ask your guardian angel to take care of it. God does not mind distractions. It is the love with which we return our focus to him that he desires. Many find it helpful to use a small notebook or journal to help focus their prayer times.

Do not overidealize your prayer. Most of the time, it won't "feel" perfect or life changing. There will be unexpected interruptions, dryness, distractions, and other things that interfere. You will experience seasons of both joy and struggle in prayer. After a prayer time, resist the temptation to evaluate "how it went." Just be faithful, and over time you will grow in your ability to pray and to follow the subtler promptings of the Spirit throughout your day.

3

Abiding in God's Word

Biblical inspiration is an inspired interworking of grace and human freedom.

Breath of God

Catholic Tradition proclaims with 2 Timothy 3:16 and with all Christians that Sacred Scripture "is inspired by God." What does this mean?

The Greek word behind "inspire" here means "to breathe or blow into." The rich Hebrew word for "spirit"—*ruah*—is the "mighty wind" hovering over the abyss at creation (Genesis 1:2, NABRE), as well as God's "breath of life" breathed into humanity in Genesis 2:7. The resurrected Jesus "breathed on" his disciples and told them, "Receive the Holy Spirit" (John 20:22).

Thus the Scriptures are "God breathed"—filled with the very life, message, and presence of God.

What does divine inspiration *not* mean? The Church's understanding of biblical inspiration is a strong rejection of other views. The Bible is *not*

1. merely a human text.

2. dictated word-for-word by God to humans acting as puppets.

Biblical inspiration is an inspired interworking of grace and human freedom. "God is its principal author, with the writer as the human collaborator. Thus the Scriptures are the word of God in human language."[8]

These four steps broadly show the Bible's origin:

1. People experienced God—from Abraham, to Moses, David, Elijah, and many others. The experience of God and of divine revelation culminated in Jesus Christ.

2. People shared verbally (in an oral tradition) their stories of these experiences with God.

3. Divinely-inspired authors collected, wrote down, and edited the stories (written tradition).

4. The early Church determined the official list (canon) of writings, which constitute those texts authentically inspired by God.

The result is a library of seventy-three writings covering diverse genres, compiled over centuries and spanning various contexts. Of these writings, forty-six were sacred texts from the Jewish heritage (Christians call these the Old Testament), and twenty-seven of them were written in response to the revelation of God in Jesus' life, death, and resurrection (the New Testament).

Because of the Church's authority to safeguard, interpret, and hand down divine revelation, the Catholic disciple can trust that, properly understood, the Bible is free from error in matters relating to faith and morals. This does not mean that the Bible answers every question, but the Bible does contain the saving good news the Lord wished to reveal.

Is Scripture True?

In Part 2, we practiced *lectio divina* and meditating on Scripture. Now let's go deeper in exploring Scripture.

Think of the rich and multifaceted ways we communicate—writing, speech, facial expressions, tone, poetry, numerical statistics, music (with or without words), art, or dance. Even packing a child's lunch can communicate love, care, and provision. Modes of communication convey meaning according to the confines of their genre and in relationship with the culture of the communicator and his or her hearers. When we ask about the truth in Scripture, all these dynamics play a part.

So do we take the Bible literally?

The Bible is not a book; the Bible is a library. So the question is, "Do you take the library literally?" Well, it depends on what section you're in! If you go in the journalism section or you go into the strict history section, yeah, you take that pretty straightforwardly. But if you wander into the poetry section or you wander into a section about mythology or you wander into a section about political opinion, then it depends on what genre you're dealing with. The Bible is not "a book"; it's a collection of books from a wide variety of literary genres. Therefore, you have to know which lenses to wear. So some books of the Bible are more straightforward; they are more historical. Think of the books dealing with David and Solomon and so on; you have the Gospels that do purport to be historical reportage. Then you have books like the beginning of the Book of Genesis, or you have the story of Jonah, and these aren't straightforward, journalistic accounts of things that happened. They are theologically rich narratives and poems. Therefore, I don't approach those with the same clunky lenses on that I use to read more historical texts. So it's a basic principle of biblical interpretation that you have to look at the genre you're dealing with.[9]

Most Catholic study Bibles contain introductions to each book of the Bible, as well as footnotes to help the non-scholar understand the trickier genres and cultural motifs.

Principles for Catholic Interpretation

Remember how biblical inspiration is an inspired interworking of grace and human freedom? "To interpret Scripture correctly, the reader must be attentive to what the human authors truly wanted to affirm and to what God wanted to reveal to us by their words."[10]

The *Catechism* lays out three principles for interpreting Scripture:[11]

1. "*Be especially attentive 'to the content and unity of the whole Scripture.'* Different as the books which *compose* it may be, Scripture is a unity by reason of the unity of God's plan, of which Christ Jesus is the center and heart, open since his Passover."

2. "*Read the Scripture within 'the living Tradition of the whole Church.'*"

3. "*Be attentive to the analogy of faith.* By 'analogy of faith' we mean the coherence of the truths of faith among themselves and within the whole plan of Revelation."

We could summarize these principles by saying that we do not only read a line or book of Scripture in isolation and try to grasp its full meaning. While we do believe that God can (and does) speak to us in a simple, direct way through any line of Scripture, a fuller grasp of the rich meanings of Scripture comes when we also keep in mind the whole of divine revelation, which encompasses the entire Bible and the Tradition of the Church.

We need not become experts in Scripture and Tradition in order to tap into the power of God's word, but as we encounter challenging questions and puzzling passages, we can be assured that more clarity emerges from the broader view of Scripture and Tradition. Catholic pastors, teachers, scholars, and resources can help aid our study as we seek answers to our most pressing questions. Yet we must bathe all of these pursuits in prayer; even scholars and "experts" stand before God in the same relationship that characterizes all of us—as beloved daughters and sons.

The Four Senses of Scripture

The early Church Fathers taught about four "senses" of Scripture that can help us understand and apply biblical truths. Understanding the senses of Scripture is a practical way to apply the principles of Catholic interpretation. Here is a brief introduction to this helpful ancient teaching.

The **literal sense** is the meaning of the text at face value. It uncovers the text's meaning in the time and place it was originally composed.

The three **spiritual senses** seek additional meanings or applications, which may be beyond the scope of the text's original context. The spiritual senses reach beyond the space, time, and consciousness of the historical human author, because God can weave together a picture much larger than any one story or time period can convey.

The literal and spiritual senses of Scripture are never opposed to one another; they analyze the text from different angles.

The next sections share a bit more detail on the literal and spiritual senses.

The Literal Sense

The literal sense of Scripture is the meaning the sacred author intended to convey at the time of the writing. It does not mean, as the word "literal" might seem to suggest, that all the words are to be taken literally. Faithful use of the literal sense means interpreting figurative texts (like poetry) figuratively, as Bishop Barron helped us to see a few pages earlier.

The more we can understand what the author intended in a text, the more we will be on track to understanding its deeper (spiritual) meanings. That is why the *Catechism* states that "all other senses of Sacred Scripture are based on the literal."[12]

The literal sense is often rather clear and obvious. In the narratives of Israel's history, for example, the literal sense simply refers to the events themselves. Moses led the people across the Red Sea as the Lord parted the waters. David committed adultery with Bathsheba. Jesus healed a blind man.

It can be a bit trickier when the text was not intended to be a simple history. The six-day creation account in Genesis 1, for example, is Hebrew poetry. It does not claim to recount a precise historical record of what happened in six twenty four-hour periods. People who conclude that dinosaurs never existed and that people arrived on the planet within an actual week of the formation of the earth are misinterpreting the literal sense of Genesis 1. The author of Genesis was not writing with post-Enlightenment historical and scientific assumptions or aims. Instead, he was conveying timeless theological truths about God, creation, and humanity. Hence, the literal sense of the early chapters of the Book of Genesis points to the following types of conclusions:

There is one all-good Creator God who created all things.

Creation is good, not evil.

God created peacefully, not as a result of violence (as in so many of the rival creation myths of the time, stemming from different nations and cultures).

Humanity is the crowning creation, endowed with gifts (like intellect and free will) that allow them to be more like

God than any other part of creation. Humans also have certain responsibilities that correspond with this gift of being like God.

The Spiritual Senses

There are three spiritual senses of Scripture:

The Allegorical Sense

Have you ever watched a movie multiple times? After learning the ending of a story, other parts become clearer. You notice foreshadowing here, details there, and shades of subtler meaning you missed the first time. The screenwriter or director probably had these in mind all along.

A similar thing happens when we view passages while knowing the "end" (or fulfillment) of the story—that is, the life, death, and resurrection of Jesus. The allegorical sense of Scripture seeks to find additional layers of meaning that come into focus when we view them through the lens of Jesus and all he revealed. The *Catechism* calls this their "significance in Christ." For example, "the crossing of the Red Sea is a sign or type of Christ's victory and also of Christian Baptism."[13] As the Israelites were freed from physical slavery through the waters of the Red Sea, so are Christians freed from the spiritual slavery of sin through the waters of Baptism.

The allegorical sense—also called the Christological sense—ties together the Old and New Testaments; as the maxim of the Church Fathers states, "The New Testament lies hidden in the Old and the Old Testament is unveiled in the New."[14]

The Moral Sense

"The events reported in Scripture ought to lead us to act justly. As St. Paul says, they were written 'for our instruction.'"[15]

We can ask "application questions" of Scripture. What does this passage teach me about how to live? Reading the moral sense in Scripture, we respond as students and servants: "Teach me your way, O LORD" (Psalm 86:11, NRSV) and "What then shall we do?" (Luke 3:10).

The Anagogical Sense

"We can view realities and events in terms of their eternal significance, leading us toward our true homeland."[16]

Anytime we gain insights from Scripture about our journey toward heaven, the divergent paths of good and evil, and the nature of the kingdom of God, we are reflecting within the anagogical sense.

Action Step: Use the Four Senses

We can seek the four senses of Scripture by asking the following questions of a biblical text:

1. What is its meaning at face value? What did it mean to the original author and hearers? [literal sense]

2. How does it point to Jesus? Or how does the Creed further illuminate its meaning? [allegorical/Christological sense]

3. How does it instruct us to live, either directly or by implication? [moral sense]

4. What does it reveal about eternal life? [anagogical sense]

Not every passage, story, or book of Scripture will present ready answers to all of these questions. It's the joyful task of the prayerful reader to ponder these questions with the help of the Holy Spirit and to respond to the Lord's voice whenever he hears it. "O that today you would hearken to his voice! / Harden not your hearts" (Psalm 95:7-8).

You don't have to be an expert.

Helpful as these senses, principles, and methods may be, the danger is that we become either too engrossed in study (and so leave *lectio divina* behind) or too intimidated by the text (and so leave *lectio divina* behind). Here's the key: Don't leave *lectio divina* behind!

To review the method of *lectio divina*, see the practice in Part 2. Let the simple method of Read, Reflect, Respond, and Rest be the hallmark of your prayerful encounters with God's word. The four senses may add some texture and depth to your *lectio*, especially the "reflect" portion, but don't let them pull you away from the intimacy of sitting with God.

If there are persistent themes you feel drawn to study more seriously, you can do that as a separate discipline from your prayer times. Be patient; it's not about answering all your questions and interpreting every sentence correctly. It's more about growing in openness to the God who inspired these texts and who is with you as you ponder them prayerfully.

With the tools of *lectio divina* and the four senses of Scripture, you can fruitfully make reading and praying with Scripture a part of your daily spiritual diet.

As Benedict XVI exhorted, "We must train people to read and meditate on the word of God: this must become their staple diet."[17]

4

Relentlessly Together

Real community is hard. It's messy.
That's how people are.

People Are Messy

Real community is hard. It's messy. That's how people are.

We concoct those images of the perfect family, Church community, government, or school. We sit in our armchairs and wish others would "do better" or "be better."

The early Church at Corinth knew a thing or two about this wishing and the difficulty of community. St. Paul directed his first letter at that community because "it has been reported to me by Chlo e's people that there is quarreling among you" (1 Corinthians 1:11).

The Corinthians quarreled about eating foods sacrificed to pagan idols, appropriate hairstyles during prophecy, and the proper procedure for celebrating Mass as a community.[18] They set up allegiances—those who belonged to Paul, others to Apollos, others to Cephas, etc. They gave each other labels—wise, simple, spiritual, strong, weak. Those well-to-do in the community started a pre-Mass party of eating and drinking instead of waiting for the day laborers to arrive ("[O]ne goes hungry and another becomes drunk. What! Do you not have homes to eat and drink in? Or do you show contempt for the church of God and humiliate those who have nothing? . . . [M]y brothers and sisters, when you come together to eat, wait for one another. If you are hungry, eat at home . . ."[19]). The Corinthians weren't living as a true community, and St. Paul called them out: don't cause division where there should be communion!

While some of the Corinthians' quarrels sound antiquated to us, Catholic communities continue to embroil themselves in squabbles just like these. St. Paul's encouragement to the Corinthians to overcome their divisions and strive toward unity in diversity applies to us: "For just as the body is one and has many members, and all the members of the body, though many, are one body, so it is with Christ" (1 Corinthians 12:12).

Yes, it's easy to wish things were different. But God asks more of us.

- How do you respond to fellow Catholics who pray, look, sing, or think differently than you?

- How do you overcome the temptation to judge or take sides?

- Are there roads to greater unity that you could pursue?

One Another

The New Testament holds numerous practical commands on how the Christian community should relate to one another. These "one another" commands often use the Greek word *allélón*, meaning roughly (surprise!) "one another." This word appears one hundred times in ninety-four New Testament verses.

About one-third of the one-another commands address unity in the Church. Things like:

- "Be at peace with one another" (Mark 9:50).

- Don't grumble among one another (see John 6:43).

- Accept one another (see Romans 15:7).

- "Wait for one another" before beginning the Eucharist (1 Corinthians 11:33).

- "Be kind to one another, tenderhearted, forgiving one another (Ephesians 4:32).

- "Confess your sins to one another" (James 5:16).

One-third of the one-another commands remind Christians to love one another. Things like:

- "Love one another."[20]

- Tolerate one another in love (see Ephesians 4:2).

About fifteen percent of the commands stress humility, like:

- Regard one another as more important than yourselves (Philippians 2:3)

- "Serve one another" (Galatians 5:13).

- "Wash one another's feet" (John 13:14.

And then we get things like:

- Do not judge one another, and don't put a stumbling block in a brother's way (see Romans 14:13).

- Speak truth to one another (see Ephesians 4:25).

- "Do not lie to one another" (Colossians 3:9).

- Spur one another on to love and good deeds (see Hebrews 10:24).

- "Pray for one another" (James 5:16).

That last one hits exactly what we are discussing here with evangelization and community: pray for one another.

As hard as it can be sometimes, we are called to pray for one another.

A Harsh and Dreadful Thing

Sitting in an armchair and wishing the world looked different is easy, but it won't give us the truth. And it won't show us the splendor of reality.

Fyodor Dostoyevsky famously captured the complexities of human nature in his novels. In *The Brothers Karamazov*, he touched on the distinction between the real and the imagined: "Love in action is a harsh and dreadful thing compared to love in dreams."[21]

- **When have you experienced "love in action" as a difficult, at times painfully "harsh and dreadful thing"? When have you been disillusioned by the demands of love? Do you find yourself thinking, "I never thought it would be this hard"?**

- **How do the struggles, which come to mind now as you think about these questions, relate to your experience of your church community? What about to your community as a whole (family, school, work, neighborhood)?**

So Annoying!

Kendra

"But I say to you, Love your enemies and pray for those who persecute you."
—Matthew 5:44

What about those who make me want to pull my hair out? I feel persecuted by how often they pinch my last nerve, but they aren't exactly enemies.

Opting for God's mission to further his kingdom on earth means I am all in for every soul, including my pesky neighbor who leaves her trash cans out all week and my coworker who manages to find infinite ways to irritate me. Jesus calls us to a higher standard, especially when it comes to those who are hard to love.

There's no room for buried grudges and passive aggressive resentment in Jesus' mission.

It's in these very places that I can't help but recognize my shortcomings. My love is flighty. My prayers are circumstantial. I am weak.

St. Paul writes in 2 Corinthians 12:9, "[B]ut he said to me, 'My grace is sufficient for you, for my power is made perfect in weakness.' I will all the more gladly boast of my weaknesses, that the power of Christ may rest upon me."

My weakness lies in my imperfect conditional love that fails to look beneath the surface. It takes guts to go beneath the surface. Going there usually leads me to repentance because in the time I spend magnifying another's weakness, I manage to overlook my own.

This mission we are called to is hard. It's humbling. Sometimes it feels crazy, even too much, but isn't that the gist of the gospel message? Welcoming the tax collector, dining with outcasts, and forgiving the unforgivable.

Jesus never said it would be easy, but he promised it would be worth it.

Are you in?

Real Community

Love is patient, love is kind.
—1 Corinthians 13:4, NABRE

So begins the favorite passage of weddings everywhere. The words are so familiar; do you dismiss them as cheesy or trite?

Though often applied to romantic love, St. Paul's treatise on love was originally written to that divided community in Corinth we've been discussing. Look closely at what St. Paul wrote to those Corinthians:

If I speak in the tongues of men and of angels, but have not love, I am a noisy gong or a clanging cymbal. And if I have prophetic powers, and understand all mysteries and all knowledge, and if I have all faith, so as to remove mountains, but have not love, I am nothing. If I give away all I have, and if I deliver my body to be burned, but have not love, I gain nothing.

Love is patient and kind; love is not jealous or boastful; it is not arrogant or rude. Love does not insist on its own way; it is not irritable or resentful; it does not rejoice at wrong, but rejoices in the right. Love bears all things, believes all things, hopes all things, endures all things.

Love never ends; as for prophecies, they will pass away; as for tongues, they will cease; as for knowledge, it will pass away. For our knowledge is imperfect and our prophecy is imperfect; but when the perfect comes, the imperfect will pass away. . . . So faith, hope, love abide, these three; but the greatest of these is love. (1 Corinthians 13:1-10, 13)

The community at Corinth thought pretty well of themselves, but St. Paul reminded them that they were nothing if they did not have love. His words, though, are not only for the Corinthians. He encourages us to love one another as well. To let love cut through any impatience or self-righteousness or envy or irritation that living life in community can bring. As Jesus had taught, they were to "love one another as I have loved you" (John 15:12).

Paul puts aside that gap between the real and the ideal and asks us to see the value and the wonder of the world as it is before us. We don't need the armchair "ideal" anymore. The "ideal" is within us to bring forth and share through reliance on God's grace and through "offering up" the inevitable frustrations of communal life.

Action Step: Intercede

We serve "one-another" best by beginning in prayer. In the school of prayer, Christ gives us more of his own heart for his people and reveals how, where, and with whom he is calling us to dwell in community.

There are many ways to intercede for people. We can bring the intentions of our hearts consciously to the Mass, spiritually laying them on the altar as the priest receives the offerings of bread and the wine. We can ask Mary to intercede for them. We can add strength and concreteness to our prayers by offering up our small (or big) sufferings of the day for various intentions. Instead of ranting aloud or fuming internally, we can ask for the grace to endure this particular cross and offer our sufferings in conjunction with a prayer for someone else's good.

A doctor friend once told me he offers each appointment of his workday for some person he wants to lift up in prayer. He actually writes the name of the person in his appointment book, next to the patient's name—what a wonderful way to turn work into intercession!

We need not understand *how* prayer works or *why* certain prayers seem to go unanswered—indeed, we cannot always understand the workings of grace. But pray we must, as Jesus commanded us to do and as Scripture exhorts time and again.

Let's pray for someone now for five or ten minutes.

Here are some questions to inspire your prayer. Pray aloud if that feels right. Sometimes praying out loud makes it easier for us to receive the words the Spirit gives us. If any specific insights or thoughts come to mind for this person you're praying for or for yourself in relation to that person, write them down so that you can return to them at another prayer time.

Begin by praying something similar to the following in your own words:

"Jesus, thank you for bringing to mind *(person's name)*. You know the heart of your beloved child, *(name)*, and you want him/her to know your love. Please make my heart as full of love and care for *(name)* as your heart is. Help me see him/her as you do. Holy Spirit, guide my prayer for *(name)*."

Think about what you know of this person. What needs does he or she have?

What might be in the way of *(name)* knowing the great love that Jesus has for him or her?

What healing, deliverance, or encouragement might this person need from the Lord?

Ask, "Holy Spirit, have I been Jesus to *(name)*? Please form in my heart your compassion for *(name)*. Jesus, I want to see through your eyes and feel through your heart for this person."

Pray, "Holy Spirit, please guide all my interactions with *(name)*, that I could be the fragrance of Christ to him/her (see 2 Corinthians 2:14-16). Please lead me to deliberately seek personal contact with him/her."

Pray, "God, you have given *(name)* an innate need and desire for you. Help him/her respond to that need and follow your promptings. If he/she doesn't know you and is filling his/her life with what can only lead him/her away from you, God, don't let these activities dull the godly restlessness that can only be satisfied by you."

Thank God for the ways he has led and inspired you during your prayer time. Tell Jesus that you trust him to show you how to be intentional with this person. Ask him for his help to be faithful with the inspirations he has given you and to follow through with the ideas for actions that he has given you.

5

A Sacramental Life

The sacraments transform not only bread, wine, and water into effective sacramental signs; they little by little transform us into Christ.

Sacramental Transformation

In Part 2, we talked about the difficulties of "defining" the sacraments and explored some basic concepts about the sacraments, especially the sacraments of the Holy Eucharist and Reconciliation. Now we will take up some of the tougher questions and ask: Where do the sacraments fit in the life of a disciple?

Let's put some concepts on the table:

Jesus is the primordial sacrament of God's presence. Said another way, Jesus is the first, truest, and most sacramental sacrament of all. Why? Because Jesus makes the invisible presence, love, mercy, and *person* of God visible to us. As the God-man, Jesus is what he signifies. He is the revelation of God.

The Church is the fundamental sacrament of Jesus' presence. When the Holy Spirit comes upon the disciples at Pentecost, they become the body of Christ. The Church that proclaims salvation also offers salvation through the sacraments.[22]

Thus the *Catechism* teaches that "**sacraments are 'powers that come forth' from the Body of Christ,** which is ever-living and life-giving. They are actions of the Holy Spirit at work in his body, the Church. They are 'the masterworks of God' in the new and everlasting covenant."[23]

The seven sacraments immerse us in the life of Christ. Through Jesus' presence in the Church, we are made *children* of God in Baptism, *messengers* of God at Confirmation, and the *body* of God in the celebration of the Eucharist. Our wounds of sickness and sin are healed in the Anointing of the Sick and in Reconciliation, and we are Christ to one another in the Sacraments of Holy Orders and Matrimony. The sacraments transform not only bread, wine, and water into effective sacramental signs; they little by little transform us into Christ.

Child of God (Baptism)

Andrea

"Why do you want your child baptized?" I sat across from Justine, expecting one of the usual answers: "I want her to know right from wrong," "It's important to our family," or "We want to pass on our faith to her."

But Justine was silent.

I looked up from my notepad. Justine trembled slightly as she gazed out the window. Holding her breath, she clasped her fingers tightly together, like she was willing calmness into the room.

"I was never supposed to get pregnant," she said. "The doctors told us it was impossible, but me and my mom started this tradition. Every morning, we'd visit a little chapel downtown and beg God for a baby. Then, about a year ago, it happened. I was pregnant." Finally, she faced me. "I want to baptize my daughter because I know she is a gift from God. She belongs to him."

Can you imagine how deeply God longs for you? He is a good Father. He desires you as his child. "[The Father] chose us in [Christ], before the foundation of the world, to be holy and without blemish before him. In love he destined us for adoption to himself through Jesus Christ, in accord with the favor of his will, for the praise of the glory of his grace that he granted us in the beloved" (Ephesians 1:4-6, NABRE).

Jesus is God's beloved and only begotten Son,[24] but through the grace of Baptism, God *adopts us*. We are made *children of God*. Can you imagine? We *belong* to God.

To Live His Life

As we reflect upon our adoption to the status of the Father's children through Baptism, recall the section in Part 1 "Being Transformed" on the remarkable journey of "deification" we're all invited to join. Saying we are God's children is saying a lot more than that we all originate from God, which could be equally said of a rock or a tree. Unlike rocks and trees (wonderful as they are), we humans may, by the grace of Baptism, "become partakers of the divine nature" (2 Peter 1:4).

What does this mean?

The *Catechism*, drawing on wisdom from the early Church, paints this sharing of the divine life as a mystical union with Christ, through which we participate in the very life Jesus lived (and lives) for us. Reflect prayerfully today on this truly remarkable claim.

> Christ enables us *to live in him* all that he himself lived, and *he lives it in us*. . . . We are called only to become one with him, for he enables us as the members of his Body to share in what he lived for us in his flesh as our model: "We must continue to accomplish in ourselves the stages of Jesus' life and his mysteries and often to beg him to perfect and realize them in us and in his whole Church. . . . For it is the plan of the Son of God to make us and the whole Church partake in his mysteries and to extend them to and continue them in us and in his whole Church. This is his plan for fulfilling his mysteries in us."[25]

- **What events in your life might you view through the lens of living out that which Christ himself lived?**

- **Have you been rejected in some way? Have you wept with someone else who was weeping, or rejoiced with someone rejoicing? Have you instructed the ignorant? Have you helped someone to see a situation more clearly? Have you had holy desires and repeated attempts to bless others** that have gone unnoticed, or even ended up scorned and misinterpreted? Do you long to reach someone in danger of making big mistakes, but you're unable to penetrate their coldness of heart toward you or toward God? Have you felt abandoned by close friends in your darkest hour?

- In these or other ways, can you see not only some ups and downs of life but graced moments of living the very life of Christ? Take heart! "He lives it in [you]"![26]

The sacraments assist us in various ways as we live this one life of Christ and grow in oneness with him.

Rescued (Eucharist)

Observe the month of Abib by keeping the Passover of the LORD, your God, since it was in the month of Abib that the LORD, your God, brought you out of Egypt by night. You shall offer the Passover sacrifice from your flock and your herd to the LORD, your God, in the place the LORD will choose as the dwelling place of his name. You shall not eat leavened bread with it. For seven days you shall eat with it only unleavened bread, the bread of affliction, so that you may remember as long as you live the day you left the land of Egypt; for in hurried flight you left the land of Egypt. (Deuteronomy 16:1-3, NABRE)

When we remember the Last Supper, the first celebration of the Eucharist, we honor and adore the miracle of Jesus transforming our simple gifts into his glorious Body.

In remembering this celebration, though, it is easy to forget the *type* of bread he lifted, blessed, broke, and shared: the bread of affliction and captivity.

Captives ate the Passover bread. Slaves preparing for escape ate that bread. The Eucharist is the Bread of Angels *and* the Bread of Affliction. Eat this bread, "the bread of affliction, so that you may remember as long as you live the day you left the land of Egypt; for in hurried flight you left the land of Egypt" (Deuteronomy 16:3).

Like the Israelites, we are fugitives, fleeing a reign of sin and death. The Light of the Nations leads us in the night. We follow through the darkness, sustained by the Bread of Affliction until we reach the land of promise. "Do this in remembrance of me" (Luke 22:19). *Remember* the day you fled Egypt and fled captivity. *Remember* the day you were freed. *Remember* who freed you.

Give thanks.

This bread is the Bread of Thanksgiving and the Bread of Remembrance. He freed us, and we have escaped. Yet we are *still* escaping the land where we were held captive, the land of our enslavement. When we eat the Bread of Affliction, we remember and we give thanks because we truly have been freed from our captors, rescued in the dark, and saved for a glorious new day.

At the Service of Communion (Holy Orders and Matrimony)

Remember our previous reflections in chapter 4, "Relentlessly Together," on the concrete challenges of community? Certain sacraments contribute in a unique way to this messy, real, and beautiful communal life. They point us to the ideal of communion while also refining our imperfect love through practice, sacrifice, and commitment.

Holy Orders and Holy Matrimony carry the special distinction of being sacraments in the service of communion. The *Catechism* says that "Holy Orders and Matrimony are directed towards the salvation of others; if they contribute as well to personal salvation, it is through service to others that they do so. They confer a particular mission in the Church and serve to build up the People of God."[27]

The vocation inherent to every human being is to love.[28] Likewise, every Christian is baptized into Jesus' priestly character—able to offer prayers and sacrificial offerings to God. So what do marriage and ministerial priesthood add to "build up the People of God"?

The priest "begets" new Christians as he baptizes them into new life. In his prayers, provision of the sacraments, and fatherly concern for those in his care, he is charged with raising all the baptized to full maturity in their baptismal graces of faith, hope, and charity. "The ministerial priesthood is at the service of the common priesthood. It is directed at the unfolding of the baptismal grace of all Christians."[29]

In some ways, the lay faithful come to their priests as little children, unable to feed themselves, needing Father to put the food of the sacraments on the table. In other ways, the priest is the father of adult children: supporting, encouraging, and exhorting the laity to live in a manner worthy of the gospel and also enjoying a mutuality and shared exhilaration of serving in God's vineyard together, ordained and lay, each according to their part in the whole.

Married couples are a sacramental sign to the community of God's faithful love for his people. "Since God created . . . man and woman, their mutual love becomes an image of the absolute and unfailing love with which God loves man. It is good, very good, in the Creator's eyes."[30]

Just as with life in general, living one's vocation as a priest or a spouse involves a gap between the real and the ideal. Recognizing the value of pouring ourselves into the *real* helps us lay aside those armchair idealizations and dig into the messy beauty of *the thing* of life, to live out those "one another" commands and to find God's graceful "ideal" within ourselves. Living within this "one another" vision of reality also helps provide a picture to others of what the world will be when we allow God's grace into our hearts.

Standing on Calvary (Anointing)

Stan wasn't getting any better. Not many people in his advanced oncology unit were. Cancer had moved in months before and was taking more ground without consideration for how Stan felt about the whole business. The hard, small beads of his rosary made crater-shaped impressions on his palm, the red coloring beginning to fade from their over-rubbed surfaces.

> Faith in the face of sickness and death can seem impossible. "In an age like our own, marked in part by the quest for instant relief from suffering, it takes special courage to stand on Calvary. Uniting our suffering with that of Jesus, we receive strength and courage, a new lease on life, and undaunted hope for the future."[31]

The sacrament of the Anointing of the Sick continues Jesus' ministry of healing to those suffering from sickness and infirmity. Anyone dealing with serious illness can ask for the sacrament to receive strength and pray for healing, whether or not death is imminent. "But [Christ] did not heal all the sick. His healings were signs of the coming of the Kingdom of God. They announced a more radical healing: the victory over sin and death."[32] Correspondingly, the sacrament's hoped-for effect is physical healing, but even if the person does not recover, the sacrament strengthens the recipient to face the difficulties and despair that can accompany serious illness.[33]

Stan's body did not overcome the cancer killing it, but the Sacrament of the Anointing of the Sick gave him hope and peace more powerful than any disease. The fear he had experienced began to dissipate, and he felt assured that Christ would carry him through every obstacle—even death.

Ultimately, faith in Jesus' total resurrection healing is the only promise that provides hope enough to face death. But the One who "took our infirmities and bore our diseases" (Matthew 8:17) comes alongside us in life's brokenness and difficulty, allowing us to say with the psalmist, "I believe I shall see the LORD's goodness / in the land of the living. / Wait for the LORD, take courage; / be stouthearted, wait for the LORD!" (Psalm 27:13-14, NABRE).

Sealed and Sent (Confirmation)

Have you ever noticed the word "sent" in the Bible? Start looking and you'll find it everywhere! Jesus is sent by the Father to proclaim the kingdom. Jesus sends out the Twelve and the seventy-two. He sends them the Holy Spirit. And then, well, the Holy Spirit is *really* into sending. In fact, the Spirit *drives* Jesus into the desert and sends the disciples all over the place.

> While they were worshiping the Lord and fasting, the Holy Spirit said, "Set apart for me Barnabas and Saul for the work to which I have called them." Then after fasting and praying they laid their hands on them and sent them off. (Acts 13:2-3)

The Twelve were first called "disciples," or "students," of Jesus. But later, they were called the apostles. Why? An apostle is one who is *sent,* and the Twelve received a lot of sending . . . to all the edges of the known world.

> "But you shall receive power when the Holy Spirit has come upon you; and you shall be my witnesses in Jerusalem and in all Judea and Samaria and to the end of the earth" (Acts 1:8).

The Sacrament of Confirmation has two main signs: anointing with oil and laying on of hands. Both confirm or seal the graces of our Baptism. "Christ" means "anointed one," and so the anointing confirms our identity as being in Christ Jesus. Laying on of hands—an ancient tradition of the Church—confers the gift of the Holy Spirit. And once that Holy Spirit gets started, well, you know the idea. Sent.

The grace of Confirmation seals your identity in Christ and sends you on a mission as a witness to the ends of the earth.

• **Where is the Holy Spirit sending you today?**

Action Step: Discern God's Presence

St. Ignatius of Loyola, the founder of the Jesuits, asked his Jesuits to practice a specific prayer technique twice daily (at noon and at the end of the day). This technique is called the Ignatian Examen.

The Examen provides an excellent means for us to increase our obedience to God's will by increasing our awareness of his presence in our lives. Because of its efficacy in this area, some refer to the Examen as the Awareness Examen or an Examination of Consciousness (not to be confused with an examination of conscience only, though such an examination may be part of the Examen). We don't need to pray it twice a day to experience the power of this great prayer practice from the Catholic Tradition.

We include this practice here, in this chapter on the sacramental life, because the seven sacraments help us further recognize the reality of God's ever-present action in our lives, even as they form and equip us to become God's presence for others. The Examen helps us to grow in discerning the subtle signs of the Lord's presence and to notice our responses to God's gentle promptings.

To practice the Ignatian Examen, proceed through the following steps. You may spend fewer than five minutes in contemplation, or you may engage in a longer meditation of ten to fifteen minutes, whichever length suits your prayer life (or a given prayer time) best.

1. **Preparation:** Take a few deep breaths and try to enter, interiorly, into a prayerful state. Put things aside, and

close your eyes. You could even cross your arms over a desk and lay your head on them. Rest. Turn your attention to God's presence. Let the busyness of the day melt away, and find that stillness we've talked so much about.

2. **Gratitude**. Recall anything from the day for which you are especially grateful, and give thanks.

3. **Review**. Recall the events of the day, from start to finish, noticing where you encountered God's presence, and where you accepted or turned away from his grace for that moment.

4. **Sorrow**. Recall any actions for which you are sorry.

5. **Forgiveness**. Ask God's forgiveness. Decide whether you need to reconcile with anyone you have hurt.

6. **Grace**. Ask God for the grace you need for the next day and an ability to see God's presence more clearly.

Different practitioners and teachers, of course, approach the Examen a bit differently. Explore different guides online. Fr. Mark Thibodeaux, SJ, has a helpful book of variations on the Examen called *Reimagining the Ignatian Examen: Fresh Ways to Pray from Your Day*,[34] which is also available for free in the form of the smartphone application, *Reimagining the Examen*.

Find a version that fits you and try using the Examen at a set time daily (or twice daily!).

6

Becoming Good News

Our body is broken. Our communion lacks these vital lost members. We need our missing brothers and sisters.

Me? Evangelize?

When you think about evangelization, what comes to mind? If you're like most of us, it's a mixed portion of fear, excitement, joy, weariness, guilt, zeal, and hope.

Most Catholics realize that we *ought* to evangelize. We see the emptying pews each week at Mass, we know the friends and relatives who have just drifted away, and we hear the homilies that exhort us to reach out. We know the power of the love and zeal within us. But really: Me? Evangelize?

Fear creeps up our sides and nestles into our consciousness, concocting reason after reason why evangelization is not really meant for *me* . . . , right?

Common fears include offending someone or saying the wrong thing, not being holy or good enough, not knowing enough, or revealing our own brokenness or insufficient faith. The truth? Boiling it down, most of us have a fear of not being enough. And you know what? We're right. We're not enough.

This fear relates to that *gap* we've been talking about all along. We know we fall short of what we *could* be. But that's where God comes in.

St. Paul, a learned Jew, a mighty communicator, full of energy and initiative, was insufficient. Yet in the face of his weaknesses, he heard Jesus say, "My grace is sufficient for you, for my power is made perfect in weakness" (2 Corinthians 12:9).

In his Second Letter to the Corinthians, St. Paul writes with a sense of wonder about who is qualified to spread the gospel. "Not that of ourselves we are qualified to take credit for anything as coming from us; rather, our qualification comes from God, who has indeed qualified us" (2 Corinthians 3:5-6, NABRE). A wise man, Paul knew that no education, training, or experience could qualify him to share the good news. His qualification for evangelization came from God.

Let Jesus speak this to your fears and insecurities: "My grace is sufficient for you. My light can shine out of your dark places. My power will be perfected in your weakness. Draw near to me. Do not lose heart. It is I who qualifies you."

Deepest Identity

Pope St. Paul VI told us that the Church "exists in order to evangelize."[35] Why?

Jesus proclaimed the kingdom of God with his words, actions, and person. He illuminated a path out of the oppression of sin and death to those who would follow him. He identified himself as the Way, the Truth, and the Life (see John 14:6).

Jesus heals the rift between how we are and how we want to be, how the world is and how it one day will be in its fullness. He bridged *the gap*. After his resurrection, he commissioned the Twelve to "go therefore and make disciples of all nations" (Matthew 28:19)—disciples, baptized into the death and resurrection of Jesus, who would follow him through hardship, joy, life, death, and into everlasting life.

Evangel is the Greek root of "evangelization." It means "good news." The additional *-ization* (the Latinate suffix) suggests a process of becoming or making into whatever root it is attached to. So *evangelization* is "**good-news-ization,**" the process of becoming the good news, like Jesus. "*[T]o evangelize* does not mean simply to teach a doctrine, but to proclaim Jesus Christ by one's words and actions, that is, to make oneself an instrument of his presence and action in the world."[36]

Thus it becomes easy to say with Pope St. Paul VI that "evangelizing is in fact the grace and vocation proper to the Church, her deepest identity."[37] If we, the Church, aren't drawing people into life-changing encounters with the person of Jesus Christ, the good news, through our actions and our words, what on earth are we doing? If we're not evangelizing, we've lost our very identity. We're not who we were meant to be.

A Fire Gives Off Heat: Works of Mercy

When the fire of the gospel burns in us, it gives off heat. This heat within us may pour out into the world in many ways.

The spiritual and corporal works of mercy provide great examples of what "good-news-izing" the world can look like, as the Father's heart overflows into the words and actions of his children. We who consume the Body of Christ and become "instrument[s] of his presence and action in the world"[38] will find a growing correlation between these lists and our daily lives.

Prayerfully and slowly reflect on these lists now.

Corporal Works of Mercy

1. Feeding the hungry
2. Giving drink to the thirsty
3. Sheltering the homeless
4. Clothing the naked
5. Visiting the sick and imprisoned
6. Ransoming the captive
7. Burying the dead

Spiritual Works of Mercy

1. Instructing the ignorant
2. Counseling the doubtful
3. Admonishing the sinner
4. Bearing wrongs patiently
5. Forgiving offenses willingly
6. Comforting the afflicted
7. Praying for the living and the dead

Identify one action from each list that Jesus is calling you to live out. Be specific in your reflections:

- **Who is one person God is calling me to share compassion with?**

- **What does living a particular work of mercy look like for and with this person?**

Don't overlook those closest to you. It can be hard to love the "unlovable" near us. It may be easier to send money to some organization that does "good works" far away (a good thing; still send that money!) than to engage in concrete actions for and with those around us.

A Heart for People

Perhaps we grew up hearing, time and again, a very important truth: God loves *all* people. We might be less accustomed to hearing that God shows special concern for *some* of his people. Isn't it against God's nature to play favorites? What do we mean by "special concern"? We need only examine Scripture to understand.

The Old and New Testaments both show that God has *special concern* for those who need the most help! That makes all the sense in the world to parents, teachers, and doctors. To the extent that anyone is lost, broken, suffering, or weak, the Lord's heart is moved with compassion.

Jesus said, "Those who are well have no need of a physician, but those who are sick; I came not to call the righteous, but sinners" (Mark 2:17). As followers of Jesus, we are at once the sick who need divine healing, as well as the physician's assistants helping restore a wounded world!

The fifteenth chapter of Luke's Gospel contains three parables featuring "lost" things: the lost sheep, the lost coin, and the lost son. We invite you to prayerfully ponder these passages in order to foster growth in sharing Christ's heart with those who need his help. In Part 2, we introduced the practice of *lectio divina*: Read, Reflect, Respond, and Rest. Take some time to read the parables of the lost sheep and the lost coin (below), and do some *divine reading* now or sometime soon.

As you consider this Scripture, ponder these questions:

- **How do these parables communicate the Father's heart to you?**

- **How do they define being lost?**

- **From your experience and the experiences of people you know, what can "lost" look like or feel like?**

- **When/where have you been the one lost? In what ways do you still need to be found?**

Read, Reflect, Respond, and Rest

Luke 15:1-10

¹ Now the tax collectors and sinners were all drawing near to hear him. ² And the Pharisees and the scribes murmured, saying, "This man receives sinners and eats with them."

³ So he told them this parable: ⁴ "What man of you, having a hundred sheep, if he has lost one of them, does not leave the ninety-nine in the wilderness, and go after the one which is lost, until he finds it? ⁵ And when he has found it, he lays it on his shoulders, rejoicing. ⁶ And when he comes home, he calls together his friends and his neighbors, saying to them, 'Rejoice with me, for I have found my sheep which was lost.' ⁷ Just so, I tell you, there will be more joy in heaven over one sinner who repents than over ninety-nine righteous persons who need no repentance. ⁸ 'Or what woman, having ten silver coins, if she loses one coin, does not light a lamp and sweep the house and seek diligently until she finds it? ⁹ And when she has found it, she calls together her friends and neighbors, saying, 'Rejoice with me, for I have found the coin which I had lost.' ¹⁰ Just so, I tell you, there is joy before the angels of God over one sinner who repents."

Missing

Evangelization happens in the context of relationship. It is the fruit of community. We experience the good news as Jesus is proclaimed to us, introduced to us, or shown to us by others. Disciples draw one another more deeply into the life of God, together following "Jesus, the leader and perfecter of faith" (Hebrews 2:12, NABRE).

When you feel the love and strength a good Catholic community provides, it is natural to want to soak it in. But do not forget those who are not present.

> "The Christian community is never closed in upon itself. The intimate life of this community . . . only acquires its full meaning when it becomes a witness, when it evokes admiration and conversion, and when it becomes the preaching and proclamation of the Good News. Thus it is the whole Church that receives the mission to evangelize, and the work of each individual member is important for the whole."[39]

In order to evangelize, we must keep following Jesus. It is he who will lead us to his dear children, weighed down under sin and darkness. He wants each of his beloved sons and daughters to know him, to love him, and to be in life-giving communion with him, their Savior.

Our community is less without these beloveds. We ought to long for these brothers and sisters of ours. Our body is broken. Our communion lacks these vital lost members. Their absence is important. Do you feel it?

So where are they? Who are they? Do you know their names? If we're going to invite them back, we must get to know them! Guess what? *Jesus already knows them.* Seek his heart and beg him to guide your steps to go out and find his lost sheep.

Jesus' People

Spiritual friendship is the environment of evangelization. The ordinary form of proclamation is face-to-face and one-on-one, in conversation. An inspiring homily or a well-written book may spur someone on, but sooner or later, that person needs to talk to another person. They need to hear the other person's experience and to be able to say, "Oh, you too?" and find a holy kinship.

If this exchange does not happen, how will the seeker know that their hopes and deep longings for God are not merely the musings of a fool or the effects of too little sleep or a bad meal? They may be tempted to write off their desires for more in this life as a personal failure rather than a call from a loving Creator who made us all for greatness. Those who are seeking God need your friendship, to hear you say, "Yes, I feel it too."

Andrea

Seekers need to meet Jesus' people. When I was dating, it was important that I meet my boyfriends' families and friends. If I didn't feel relaxed with them or couldn't have fun with them, that was a warning sign. If I was in open conflict with them or couldn't respect them, that was an even bigger issue! But if I felt at home with them, if they cared about me and my interests, if I found them interesting and admired them . . . well, halleluiah!

A person on the verge of giving their yes to Jesus has similar assessments to make. Even if they like Jesus (the "boyfriend" in this metaphor), they are going to have to meet other Catholics to get to know his "people." Introduce your friend to your own Catholic friends, especially the fellow disciples you love and trust and who give you strength. Your friend will gain a broader experience of Jesus' people from them and catch insights, ideas, perspectives, and love from how they interact with each other and with your friend.

Action Step: Make a List

Who do you know already?

Prayerfully make a list of some acquaintances, friends, colleagues, family members, . . . anyone you can think for whom the Lord might be asking you to put more thought and prayer into being part of his good news.

Go over different areas of your life.

Are there classmates, coworkers, gym acquaintances, or the person in the pew behind you every Sunday? Get them all on your list. Continue to pray over the list.

Who are two or three people the Lord is drawing you to focus on at this time?

What is one thing you could do to reach out to each of them that would deepen the ties of your relationship? Could you text someone today to go out for a beer or some ice cream? Would someone respond to the invitation to go running together? Could you orchestrate a "girls' night" or "guys' night" to have a reason to invite one of these people over and let them get to know your friends better? Could you lend someone your weed wacker?

What one thing will you do to strengthen the bonds of friendship?

PART 4

BECOME A GUIDE: LEARNING TO MAKE DISCIPLES

7

The Lord Sends Laborers

Be willing to join Jesus, who runs with you into the mission fields.

You Exist to Evangelize

Ever wonder what you're here on earth for? We all do; it's part of the great human quest. This internal inquiry relates to some of the big questions we touched on in Part 1 when we discussed *the gap*. It's natural to ask these questions.

At the most basic level, all the baptized have the same vocation: "to **holiness** and to the mission of **evangelizing** the world"(*Catechism*, 1533, emphasis added). We are here on earth to know Christ and grow in likeness to him (holiness) and to be "an instrument of his presence and action in the world" by making Christ known to others (evangelization).[40] We've hit on these ideas throughout the exploration we've been doing here together.

As a member of the Church, the same things said of the Church are true of you. Put your name in the blanks (where the Church and papal documents state "the Church"), and try reading aloud this passage:

> We wish to confirm once more that the task of evangelizing all people constitutes the essential mission of _____ . . . . Evangelizing is in fact the grace and vocation proper to _____, [his]/her deepest identity. [He]/She exists in order to evangelize.[41]

> In the broad sense, [evangelization] sums up _____'s entire mission: [his]/her whole life consists in . . . the proclamation and handing on of the Gospel.[42]

- **What is your reaction?**

- **What do such claims mean to you?**

A Sending God

Throughout Scripture, God sends on mission those who encounter him. Adam and Eve are commissioned both to "be fruitful and multiply" (Genesis 1:22) and to "till [the garden] and keep it" (2:15). Abraham is sent to a new and distant land to begin a family of God's chosen people and to learn the Lord's ways amidst people who worship false gods (see chapter 12). Moses encounters the Lord in the burning bush and is subsequently sent to free the Israelites from slavery (see Exodus 3). The prophets each receive their call to preach God's words to wayward ears, even at great cost to their own safety and comfort.

We see this pattern even more clearly when Jesus steps onto the stage: "Come to me" (Matthew 11:28), "Follow me" (4:19), and "I send you out" (Luke 10:3).

All disciples are missionary disciples. All who follow are sent because we follow a sending God—a God of mission.

What we all must come to grips with, even if we'll never sufficiently understand it, is that God chooses to involve imperfect, incomplete, not-yet fully transformed people (us) to do his "good-news-izing" work. Part of God's plan for our own grace-filled transformation involves helping others in their grace-filled transformation.

We might be tempted to think that God could be more efficient at saving the world if he would just swoop down and bring all things into accord with his will once and for all. But he has not chosen to act this way. He wills to teach, to guide, and to accompany us in doing his will in the face of fierce resistance—both from within and outside of ourselves. Like any good parent, God wants his children to grow up, to mature, and to join him in the battle for all that is good, true, and beautiful.

A Unique Task

Another word for *evangelization* is "apostolate," which stems from the word "apostle," or "one who is sent." It means mission. The Church defines "apostolate" as all activity directed toward "**spreading the kingdom of Christ throughout the earth for the glory of God the Father,**" that "**the whole world might enter into a relationship with Christ.**"[43]

Recall your fundamental vocation to holiness and evangelization. Your mission—your apostolate—is to do your part in bringing others "into a relationship with Christ."

This mission is not accomplished by accident. More is needed than going to church and trying to be a good person. Remember (in Part 1, "Being Transformed") discussing how being "Mr. Nice Guy" isn't enough? The apostolate requires the great intentionality and zeal of a focused missionary. Pope St. John Paul II clarifies that, within this universal apostolate of the Church, "each member of the lay faithful" is "**entrusted with a unique task which cannot be done by another.**"[44] There may be some people who have yet to experience a living relationship with Christ, whom *only you* can reach!

If you feel a bit unworthy for this task, you're in good company! Those whom God called in Scripture had many "buts" when they first heard about what God wanted to do through them:

Like Moses: "But I'm not a good public speaker!" "But who am I to go to Pharaoh?" "But what shall I tell them when they ask me your name?" "But don't you have the wrong guy?" (see Exodus 3).

And Jeremiah: "But I'm too young!" (see Jeremiah 1:6).

And Peter: "But I'm a sinful man!" (see Luke 5:8).

They grasped at least some of the magnitude of their calling.

- **Do you grasp the magnitude of your call to the apostolate—to evangelize?**

- **What are your "buts"?**

A Clash of Kingdoms

Where are we in the story of the Lord's saving plan?

Here's a news flash: we're not yet at the part where God simply wins. That day will come. It is a promise we can be assured of, thanks to the cross and resurrection of Jesus. One day, God "will wipe away every tear" (Revelation 21:4), and "every tongue [will] confess that Jesus Christ is Lord" (Philippians 2:11). But that day has not yet come.

Sin and death still reign in many segments of our world and our lives. Evil is at work. "The kingdom of God is at hand" (Mark 1:15), but the "ruler of this world" (John 14:30)—"the father of lies" (8:44)—is also real and exhibiting his influence. He "prowls around like a roaring lion, seeking some one to devour" (1 Peter 5:8).

So for all our love for God and confidence in his saving victory for us, let us never be naive about the battle being waged right now for every soul not yet safe in God's eternal home! "The thief comes only to steal and kill and destroy," said Jesus. "I came that they may have life, and have it abundantly" (John 10:10).

Whether we like to admit it or not, whether we think the analogy is too violent or not, the fact remains: we are at war. Our world is a clash of two kingdoms with diametrically opposed appetites and wills.

> "For we are not contending against flesh and blood, but against the principalities, against the powers, against the world rulers of this present darkness, against the spiritual hosts of wickedness in the heavenly places" (Ephesians 6:12).

Poverty, abuse, addiction, racism, sexism, human trafficking, abandonment, depression, hopelessness, and darkness of every kind are *not* God's will—but these are realities to contend with in our world. Jesus, the Divine Physician, is the only one who can heal, restore, and liberate us into the freedom God longs to give us. But he doesn't force his way and take over all at once. He gives each one of us an important role to play in our small circle of influence. He calls us to partner with him and cooperate with grace as we journey toward that ultimate victory that will one day reach completion in him.

Our call to evangelize is not simply an urging to be good, nice people who make the world a better place. We are each called to a unique task in the ongoing battle for God's kingdom to reign "on earth as it is in heaven" (Matthew 6:10).

Ready or Not

The point of the last section isn't to make us fanatical or afraid. These ideas simply remind us that a *normal* part of our Christian life and vocation is to resist evil and to "fight the good fight of the faith" (1 Timothy 6:12). This call means more than just seeking to grow in holiness. It means laying down our lives for our friends (see John 15:13), joining Jesus in radiating "the light of the world" (Matthew 5:14), and running with him, the Good Shepherd, who leaves the ninety-nine in search of the *one* who is lost and least (see Matthew 18:13; 25:31-46; John 10:11).

Let us all wake up to mission! Let us never merely sit back and wait for people to come to our churches, assuring ourselves that we are a "welcoming community." Let us pray to receive more of the Father's heart for his children who are "harassed and helpless, like sheep without a shepherd" (Matthew 9:36). After Jesus described the crowds like this, he turned his compassionate gaze to the Twelve and said, "The harvest is plentiful, but the laborers are few; pray therefore the Lord of the harvest to send out laborers into his harvest" (9:37-38). Imagine those original apostles praying for such laborers.

Are you part of the answer to their prayers?

Action Step: Declare Your Commitment

Write or speak a prayer now to the Lord of the harvest, declaring your commitment to labor with him and to fulfill your unique task in the Great Commission to "make disciples of all nations" (Matthew 28:19).

Remember, it's not your intelligence and perfection that will get the job done, but your willingness to join Jesus, who runs with you into the mission fields. Even as we seek our ongoing healing in Christ, he sends us out on his own healing mission. "And lo," he tells us, "I am with you always" (Matthew 28:20).

Finding the "Lost One"

Andre

As a husband and father, a primary way I am called to "make disciples of all nations" (Matthew 28:19) involves devoting myself to my wife and children in love, service, companionship, and leadership. But as I reflect on how to imitate the Good Shepherd, who also leaves the ninety-nine sheep in search of "the one which is lost, until he finds it" (Luke 15:4), more emerges in my calling. Surely, the "lost one" may at times be a member of my own immediate family, and there's no more important place for me to "lay down my life" than in this vocation of husband and father. But I also believe that the Lord will often place people in our lives—beyond our immediate families—for us to pursue with the heart and zeal of the Good Shepherd.

After several years of focusing primarily on loving my immediate family and just keeping my head above water trying to establish my career, I felt a growing desire to invite the Lord more explicitly (if it was his will) to use me to help reach any "lost sheep" he might lead me to accompany. I prayed to rid myself of false motives; I didn't want to develop a "savior complex" or some unhealthy "need to be needed." I prayed against pride and desires to have a flashy, "evangelical" story to tell.

The Lord let me continue praying for opportunities to "reach the lost" for a few years without any observable answers. I knew people all around me were hurting, seeking, and deeply in need of more of Jesus' light and life, but I was not gaining the type of closeness and trust required to break through the protective masks of superficiality, busyness, and personal distance we all tend to wear. God was purifying my intentions beautifully. He invited me to trust that he wanted renewal and rescue for people even more than I did. If I would continue to find my life in him, to pray and look for open doors into people's lives, he would use me in whatever ways he saw fit.

After several years of praying, serving, trusting, and slowly, naturally building relationships with other men in my professional, parish, and school communities, as well as through my kids' sports teams, the Lord opened the floodgates of the leave-the-ninety-nine-for-the-one type of apostolate in my life. One guy from a different city, with whom I was getting together occasionally on some work trips, finally leveled with me, telling me what was *really* going on in his life. Despite seeming to "have it all together" (including for his parish, kids' school, and sports teams, which continually threw leadership requests at him), he described himself as utterly lost, falling apart at the seams. Some horribly painful experiences in his past had prompted him to run hard and fast away from God for over a decade; he had been medicating his wounds with all kinds of addictive, sinful, and false comforts. He was struggling with any remaining sense of self-worth, wondering if God cared, and was tortured by all kinds of inner turmoil.

A second guy opened up to me about his failing marriage. A third guy shared with me about a painful divorce over a decade prior, which left wounds of abandonment and self-loathing that had birthed further isolation and several destructive habits. All three men were addicted to pornography and racked with shame. All three were mired in darkness beyond what is described here. And all three shared these things with me, their trusted friend, one-on-one.

To be in the presence of someone honestly sharing their true self, the story of their soul, is some of the holiest ground we can possibly stand on.

Though I was in over my head in every one of these three instances, I knew I was where the Lord wanted me to be. How was I to love, to guide, to accompany, to evangelize these brave men who dared to open their real stories to me?

The Lord calls us to leave the safety of the ninety-nine and find the one. In my case, after many years of not knowing who "the one" might be for me but praying intentionally into this call, Jesus led me to three "ones." What a humbling, difficult, messy, and beautiful call we have to imitate the Good Shepherd!

As I began walking with these men, each went at his own pace. There were many setbacks and ups and downs. I prayed with and for them, shared my own life and journey with them and, when possible, helped them to discover more of the Lord's love or the riches of the sacraments and the Church. There were moments—even seasons—when I thought I was doing everything wrong. There were times when the cost seemed too high and I wanted to give up on them. There were moments that can only be described as thick with God's overflowing grace. And all of these journeys continue in the present; they are far from over. I'm not the only one involved in these men's stories. All three have drawn upon counselors, priests, and their community. We don't walk alone, and I count it among some of my most treasured graces to be entrusted with the mission of accompanying these beautiful, hurting, and healing men. Part of my own journey of discipleship is wrapped up in this sacred accompaniment I now share with my brothers in Christ.

The lost, the least, and the lonely: it is not always obvious who or where they are. The darkness, the enemy, and the brokenness of creation are all around us. "But where sin abounded, grace did much more abound" (Romans 5:20, KJV)!

8

Person to Person

Love is the basis of all evangelization.

So *how* do we evangelize? How do we run with Jesus into the mission fields that are "ripe for harvest" (John 4:35, NIV)?

If we answer this question with mere tactics or with grandiose plans or strategies, we will miss the mark every time. What can we say about "how" to evangelize in a way that both honors the broad array of possibilities and carries meaning for all of us?

The Evangelical Catholic uses the image of a pyramid to establish three fundamental principles when beginning to answer the question of how we evangelize.

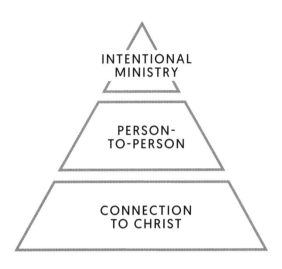

Connection to Christ is the only true foundation for our lives in Christ and for all evangelical work. "I am the vine, you are the branches," says Jesus, "for apart from me you can do nothing" (John 15:5). He is the source of all our life and love. To the extent that we grow in love for God in Christ and the Holy Spirit, we will overflow into the other levels of the pyramid.

Person-to-Person means evangelization happens most effectively within trusting relationships. As Cardinal George put it, "You cannot evangelize what you do not love."[45] Good programs, events, books, videos, and strategies can help efforts to evangelize, but *only people can love people*. Friendship is the environment of fruitful evangelization.

Intentional Ministry means putting thought into guiding and accompanying others through deepening stages of conversion and discipleship. On a "micro" level, this means helping individuals discover Christ in a life-changing way and helping them grow toward Christian maturity. On a "macro" level, it means organizing our parishes around effective methods and processes for helping people make this journey.

The Evangelization Pyramid reminds us that evangelization is about *intentionally and relationally* drawing people deeper into the abundant life of *Christ.*

The three parts of this journey we've been through so far here have focused on living your connection to Christ. This Part 4 focuses on how to draw others—relationally and intentionally—deeper into the life of Christ.

Are you ready to get personal?

People over Programs

Andre

I once served on an evangelization committee that insisted on continuing to talk (at length) about the parish website, the bulletin, and which picture of baby Jesus would appear most "welcoming" to visitors at Christmas Mass. There was also much talk of various programs we could run, curricula we could invest in, guest speakers we could invite, and huge events that drained a lot of time and effort from parish staff and volunteers. While none of these topics are bad in themselves, it became very clear that these were not the types of conversations that would lead to more effective evangelization in our community.

When it comes to evangelization, many of us tend to think big before we think small. We hope there's some magic bullet plan that will bring large numbers of people into our faith community. Or if we don't think big, then perhaps we think impersonally—as if marketing efforts, great DVDs, and websites will get the job done. What we don't often imagine is the need for each of us to engage in the persistent, *personal*, messy, uncertain, and long-range work of person-to-person accompaniment with the people God places in our lives.

Mother Teresa may have said it best:

> I don't agree with the big way of doing things. To us, what matters is an individual. To get to love the person, we must come in close contact with him. If we must wait till we get the numbers, then we will be lost in the numbers, and we will never be able to show that love and respect for the person. I believe in person to person. Every person is Christ for me, and since there is only one Jesus, there is only one person in the world for me at that moment.[46]

- **How do these words of St. Teresa of Calcutta strike you as you consider your own call to evangelize?**

People Are Not Projects

One of the reasons we might struggle with identifying as an evangelist is that we don't want to turn people into our own evangelization "projects." We all know the hypocrisy of the person who seems more interested in his or her own success and reputation than in showing genuine care and love for others.

Luckily, we need look no further than the New Testament to dispel any such misperceptions regarding evangelization. St.

Paul shows us the heart of an evangelist who does not treat his people like projects for his own gain or reputation but instead embodies the following attitude: "being affectionately desirous of you, we were ready to share with you not only the gospel of God but also our own selves, because you had become very dear to us" (1 Thessalonians 2:8).

Jesus himself treated people with deep understanding and concern, entering into their pain and joy—sometimes in countercultural ways. When others would have him shoo away the children, he says, "Let the children come to me, . . . for to such belongs the kingdom of God" (Mark 10:14). When the blind Bartimaeus calls out for healing and others try to silence him, Jesus bids him come and asks, "What do you want me to do for you?" (10:51). When Jesus gets to Bethany after Lazarus has died, the dead man's sisters meet Jesus with wails of pain, frustration, and even blame. Instead of defending himself or rushing to the miracle of raising the man from the dead, he simply shares the pain of his friends in that sacred moment: "Jesus wept" (John 11:35).

The examples of Jesus and Paul remind us that *love is the basis of all evangelization*. When we love others well, we genuinely desire that they discover the riches of life in Christ, without imposing our own agendas and schedules.

- **Who has led you closer to Jesus by loving you well and sharing their life with you?**

- **In what ways does this person's example inspire you to love others?**

Meeting People Where They Are

Andre

I spent a few glorious summers studying at the University of Notre Dame. The beauty and prayerfulness of that campus in summertime is simply stunning. One of the striking features of the campus is the sheer number of walkways that stretch through the many well-manicured lawns. An aerial view of the campus reveals just how extensive these intricate pathway webs really are.

Apparently, some of these walkways were later additions to the campus—not only because of new buildings, which required new paths, but also because students kept taking shortcuts across lawns, wearing down the grass. The university has often opted to pave these renegade paths to protect the beauty of the campus and the safety of their students.

It's also fitting that, as a Catholic University, Notre Dame features a big, beautiful basilica in the heart of campus. Many of the pathways lead to this center of worship of the One True God.

This image of the Notre Dame campus provides a fitting icon for the mission of the laity to evangelize the world. We must go out to where people are, not only where we wish people would be (on the nice, clean pathways of life or safe within the bosom of the Church). Through love, service, and genuine friendship, we must accompany others on their journey, becoming united with them in all things but sin, as Jesus did for us. Only by meeting people where they are can we hope to "make straight the way of the Lord" (John 1:23) to and with them. Let us not stay only on the paved pathways but run to wherever and whomever the Lord leads us.

- **What are some ways this metaphor speaks to you about your life?**

- **Who has left the safe paths to find and walk with you?**

- **What wayward paths in your life were eventually transformed—by Christ or those whom he sent—into pathways to God?**

- **For whom are you called to pave a path of godly friendship?**

The Art of Listening

Evangelization, of course, begins with the witness of life—living our connection to Christ. Without striving to live as disciples (though we never do it perfectly), proclaiming Christ would be hypocrisy.

But as Pope St. Paul VI reminds us, words are also necessary:

The Good News proclaimed by the witness of life sooner or later has to be proclaimed by the word of life. There is no true evangelization if the name, the teaching, the life, the promises, the kingdom and the mystery of Jesus of Nazareth, the Son of God are not proclaimed.[47]

Yet how do we use words? How do we proclaim the word of life?

Later chapters will dive into this topic further, but for now, let us consider an initial building block.

Before we ever proclaim the name of Jesus to an individual, we all have a tool readily at our disposal for using words. This tool works wonders for building bridges of friendship and leads, over time, to opportunities to speak fruitfully of the riches of Christ.

The tool we are talking about is *questions*. Love takes a reverent interest in people. And genuinely interested people ask questions. They listen deeply to the responses, and they ask more questions. We're not talking about forced, awkward, and interrogating conversations, but natural exchanges that happen in everyday life and deepen over time as relationships grow.

Evangelization has as much (or more) to do with listening as with speaking, and listening requires genuine conversation.

As missionary disciples, we (even the introverts among us!) should grow into excellent conversationalists. Jesus himself was the great asker of questions. His questions drew people out of themselves and into the deeper matters of life and faith. Consider his conversations with the Twelve (throughout the Gospels), the woman at the well (see John 4:1-29), and the men on the road to Emmaus (see Luke 24:13-35)—to name just a few.

How can we meet people where they are if we don't know where they are?

And how can we know where people are if they don't share with us their lives, their stories, and their experiences of faith?

And how will people share their stories with us if we never ask them any questions?

Love people well. Build trusting relationships with those the Lord has called you to know. Be generous and kind. Pray for people by name. Ask questions and prompt good conversations of all kinds. Many other opportunities for leading others deeper into Christ will follow from these foundational steps.

Action Step: Practice Better Conversations

Go and do it!

Today, tomorrow, this week.

With whom will you engage in proactive, natural conversation?

We're not talking about "Jesus talk" necessarily (yet)—just plain old conversation about life and everyday stuff.

Pray about how the Lord wants you to proceed. Might you:

- **Be more attentive to people at Sunday Mass and introduce yourself to someone new after the closing song?**

- **Invite a couple or a family over for dinner with no agenda other than to get to know them better and have a nice time together?**

- **Ask more questions and listen more deeply to your spouse, a child, a friend, a family member, a neighbor, a coworker, someone you find difficult, or someone else you see regularly?**

- **Follow up on a previous conversation? ("How did that test go that you told me you were worried about?")**

- Reach out to someone you haven't been in touch with as much as you believe the Lord wants?

- Handwrite and send a personal note to someone expressing good will and prayers, with a promise to call sometime soon?

Spend some time asking the Lord to identify anyone with whom he wishes you to engage in a more intentional, relational way.

Read over the following tips, which give brief reminders and practical applications of some of the content of this unit. Record your thoughts and resolutions in a journal. Surrender your fears to God, and ask for the Holy Spirit's anointing. Then, go to it!

Ten Tips for Leading Better Conversations

Good conversations build trust and friendship, and certain practices help fuel that kind of conversation.

1. Ask questions!
It takes effort, thought, and intention, but asking good questions can jump-start the flow of conversation.

2. Make *them* the expert.
Everyone is an "expert" in something and loves to talk about it. Find that thing for this person.

3. Be genuinely curious, interested, and reverent toward people.

The Grand Canyon is a smaller miracle than we quirky humans are.

4. Seek first to understand.

Everyone has a deep desire to be known and understood—including you. Sacrifice some of your desire to be known, for a bit, while you give another the dignity of being truly heard, understood, and placed at the center of attention.

5. Ask about the details.

"Tell me more about that." Who, what, where, when, why? (Ask fewer yes/no questions.)

6. Use differences as a help for conversation.

Don't simply look for things in common, and don't worry if you don't have much in common. Differences present an easy opportunity to ask more questions. "I don't know the first thing about that! Tell me more about it." Don't be afraid to ask "dumb" questions. The other person will be happy to educate you!

7. Be fully present, and truly listen.

No multitasking (bodily or mentally). No half in, half out. The person in front of you is the most important thing right now.

Even when you think of something you want to say in response, keep on listening. Avoid formulating questions and responses while the other person is talking. Let those thoughts come and go as you continue to listen.

8. Watch your body language.

Smile once in a while! Unfold those arms perhaps?

9. Win the right to be heard.

You've heard it before: people don't care what you know until they know that you care. Eventually, they may ask you some questions. Then you can talk more about yourself, your thoughts, your stories, your faith.

10. Don't argue or pontificate. Try to avoid hot-button issues early on.

If an issue comes up in which someone disagrees with the Church, your first goal need not always be to defend. It may be best to simply help the person feel heard or to find some other area of common ground. Note: empathizing with someone or causing them to feel understood is *not* the same as agreeing. To build trust, prioritize building the relationship over debating issues.

9

Sharing Your Good News

The good news isn't just a definition.
It's personal.

Stories

Andrea

People love stories.

My favorite question to ask a married couple is, "How did you meet?" Or for an engaged couple, "How did you propose?" I want to know their story! I love asking these questions because invariably they'll smile, thinking back to that fond memory, even if there's teasing or joking about how it wasn't "love at first sight."

My husband and I love telling the story of how he proposed. We saw a movie together, and then we took a walk around the campus where we had met, sharing memories from our college days. The sun was setting, so we asked a passerby to take a picture of us on the bridge we were walking along. As the stranger pressed the shutter, my husband got down on one knee and proposed. Our volunteer photographer shouted, "Oh, wow!" and doubled down on the picture taking as I said yes. We love wondering if our passerby ever tells people, "You know, one time I was walking over this bridge after work, and I ended up being a part of some couple's proposal!"

We all have important stories that shape who we are. We come from somewhere, we've overcome obstacles, we've had life-defining experiences, and we have dreams for the future: all elements of our stories.

In your experience of following Jesus, there may be many important moments or stories that shape your relationship and your life of discipleship. These stories surpass any other tools at your disposal in their ability to connect with someone who is seeking God. While people do need reasonable arguments for following Jesus (of which there are many), what people *most* value is the witness and endorsement of someone they respect. As we've discussed before, "modern man listens more willingly to witnesses than to teachers, and if he does listen to teachers, it is because they are witnesses."[48]

The First Letter of St. Peter exhorts us to "always be ready to give an explanation to anyone who asks you for a reason for your hope" (3:15, NABRE). In this unit, you'll learn how to identify and share your own witness story.

You Have a Story

We know this is true of you as well: you have received the Spirit of Christ Jesus, which brings salvation and hope; your lives are a witness of faith. Whether you were baptized as a child or joined the Church as an adult, you have a story of faith. Whether you sincerely live your faith in quiet or have a great public ministry, you have a story of faith. Whether you have a grade-school knowledge of the *Catechism* or have a theological degree, you have a story of faith.

We all have—and are—stories of faith, for through the Spirit, the Gospel of Jesus Christ takes hold of us in the proclamation of his Word, and Jesus touches us in the celebration of his sacraments. When this genuinely happens, we are all set ablaze by his love.[49]

Andrea

I can point to a handful of crucial moments in my life that led to my firm commitment to follow Christ. I'm not a convert—I was baptized, made First Eucharist, and got confirmed all on schedule. Even though I grew up in the Church, however, the invitation to follow Jesus did not penetrate my heart in a meaningful way until college. As Pope Benedict puts it, "Being Christian is not the result of an ethical choice or a lofty idea, but the encounter with an event, a person, which gives life a new horizon and a decisive direction."[50] Until I encountered Jesus in a way that gave my life "a new horizon and a decisive direction," I wasn't a disciple.

People make the commitment to follow Christ—to be *all in*—in a variety of ways. Here are three of the most common:

1. a sudden, all-at-once change of direction

2. a series of events during a season of conversion

3. continuous growth in faithfulness to Jesus from childhood into adulthood

Uncovering Your Good News

But you are a chosen race, a royal priesthood,
a holy nation, God's own people, that you may declare the
wonderful deeds of him who called you out of
darkness into his marvelous light.
—1 Peter 2:9

In Part 1, we discussed an *objective* definition of the good news. Such a definition is objective because it details truth about God's actions that is common to all Christians. We defined it as:

God, infinitely perfect and blessed in himself, in a plan of sheer goodness freely created man to make him share in his own blessed life. For this reason, at every time and in every place, God draws close to man. He calls man to seek him, to know him, to love him with all his strength. He calls together all men, scattered and divided by sin, into the unity of his family, the Church. To accomplish this, when the fullness of time had come, God sent his Son as Redeemer and Savior. In his Son and through him, he invites men to become, in the Holy Spirit, his adopted children and thus heirs of his blessed life. (*Catechism*, 1)

But the good news isn't just a definition; it's personal. In this personal aspect, we can articulate it *subjectively*. You, the *subject* of your own story, experience the just-the-facts, objective good news in a way that is entirely unique to your life.

Andrea

From experience, I know that the reality of God's call to me and his desire for closeness, Jesus' saving actions, and adoption in the Holy Spirit affect my everyday life. A relationship with God the Father, through Jesus, in the Holy Spirit, has given me deep peace, confidence, purpose, and companionship in the midst of suffering, as well as an overall fuller life. I am different because of the good news; I am changed by it and affected by it. When I talk to others about the good news, I'm going to point to these things. They are part of *my* good news.

Consider your life. How is it different because of Jesus? What does your relationship with God bring to your life? What would be missing if you didn't know Jesus or had rejected his invitation to discipleship? Write out a few words or sentences that capture how Jesus is *your* good news.

A Note on Conversion

The word "conversion" denotes some sort of transformation or change—a turnaround. In the Christian context, it means someone has turned their life toward Jesus and away from sin, through grace. It describes the first step in following Christ. Each progressive step closer to Jesus strengthens and reinforces that conversion until every part of us is fixed on him and nothing could tear us away.

When you consider your personal good news and your story of faith, you may consider how people, books, spiritual practices, events, and the Church all play a part in drawing you toward Jesus and away from sin or apathy. But as you pray about all of these things, keep asking yourself how *Jesus* is the object of your conversion. A story about how you "got more involved" or "felt at home" or "gave up partying" is only part of the story. How did those experiences convert your mind, heart, and life to Jesus?

Consider these distinctions: many people who became Catholic as an adult after being raised in another Christian denomination don't consider becoming Catholic their "conversion." In fact, they may have grown up ardently following Jesus before becoming Catholic. For many, their desire to follow Jesus more deeply and to experience him in the sacraments led them to the Catholic Church.

The Church is the irreplaceable guide to Christ in the world, but she is a sacrament of Christ—making Christ present in the world in real ways—and not Christ himself. If we are converted to the Church but do not become followers of Jesus, we are missing the point. The Church knows her vocation.

"She exists in order to evangelize" (*Evangelii Nuntiandi*, 14)—not *to* herself, but *through* herself to the One who is ever the way, the truth, and the life.

Action Step: Write Your Story

We just discussed it:

> Being Christian is not the result of an ethical choice, or a lofty idea, but the encounter with an event, a person, which gives life a new horizon and a decisive direction.[51]

• **How has an encounter (or two or three!) with Jesus given your life "a new horizon and a decisive direction"?**

1. Take some time to reflect:

   • Is there a big moment when you encountered Jesus personally and it changed your life forever? Are you conscious of a time when you first said yes to Jesus?

   • Are there smaller moments, when Jesus revealed more of himself to you or you rededicated yourself to Jesus in a new, stronger, more surrendered way?

2. In a notebook, briefly describe how you came to know Jesus for the first time or more deeply at some point in your life.

3. Next, record what you were like before that moment or period in your life. What was your life like? What things did you struggle with?

4. Finally, what were you like after that moment or period in your life? What was your life like after this encounter with Jesus? What things did you do to overcome your previous struggles? How did you grow?

5. Take some time to write a short account of these three phases: your life **before**, your encounter with **Jesus**, and your life **after** this encounter.

People open a small and precious window to your stories of faith whenever they ask "you for a reason for your hope" (1 Peter 3:15, NABRE), though they probably won't use those words! But someone might ask why you're Catholic or how you deal with the stressors and sufferings of life, or they may comment on some aspect of your faith or character. When this happens, you might have a short opportunity to share a nugget of your experience, even just thirty seconds' worth, without hijacking the conversation. If the person is interested in this nugget, they will ask for more detail, and then you can share more.

Take some time now to compose a version of your story you could share succinctly in an exchange with a friend.

10

Stages of Growth

You're a Christian, and they trust you.
It's a huge step.

The Other Side of the Equation

How does someone antagonistic to the Christian faith move from active distrust to full engagement?

In the last few chapters, we considered our call to evangelization, zeroed in on the relational (person-to-person) mode of evangelization, and articulated stories of our own moments of conversion.

So far, we have focused on preparing ourselves for the mission of evangelization. But who is on the other side of that relational equation? And within the context of friendship, how can we intentionally draw others toward a relationship with Christ?

In this unit, we introduce common stages—or thresholds—people generally experience as they journey toward initial and deepening conversion.[52] You may recognize stages you worked through in the process of your own conversion. The stages are not for labeling or judging others. Instead, the thresholds provide a grid that will help you approach the people in your life lovingly, patiently, and helpfully.

The stages also don't correspond with sacramental realities. A baptized Catholic whose life is not centered on Christ would still need to pass through many of these stages on the path to discipleship. In contrast, a person joining RCIA may already live as an intentional disciple and may pass through these stages as they consider becoming Catholic.

Progression through these stages can happen quickly or slowly. Someone might zip through three stages in an afternoon and stay put in that third stage for a decade. Most people move back and forth through the stages at various points or may need to repeat the process for individual issues of belief after an initial conversion takes place.

To effectively "become a guide" for someone going through the stages of conversion, expect to exercise what Pope Francis calls "apostolic endurance" since "evangelization consists mostly of patience and disregard for constraints of time" (*Evangelii Gaudium*, 24). As you'll see in this module, walking with people is a lengthy endeavor that requires patience, prayer, and intentionality.

Trust

Trust is the first step toward full transformation in Christ. How so? If a person hasn't met a Christian they've liked, why on earth would they want to follow Jesus?!

After all, "when trust has not yet been established, lostness feels like wise skepticism and right thinking. If Christians are fanatical and narrow-minded, keeping one's distance seems like the smartest posture to take."[53]

Many people in our country have a skewed perception of Christianity, whether due to negative media exposure or real negative experiences with Christians. The general perception many modern Americans hold is that Christians are generally judgmental, bigoted, and unkind. In our postmodern and relativistic culture, even holding the belief that there is objective truth can be interpreted as exclusionist and mean.

So what do we do? How do we break through the distrust?

We become a friend. (A *real* friend. Remember: people are *never* projects, and evangelization happens best in the context of *real* friendship.)

A person who is distrustful of your faith may still be willing to bond with you over other commonalities—a shared hobby or sport, your kids' school, or neighborhood/campus events.

One of the reasons laypeople are so valuable in the Church's mission of evangelization is that we are in the world. We can brush shoulders with those who are lost and build up credibility and trust with others.

When a person who is distrustful befriends someone who is kind, interesting, fun—heck, normal!—they may be surprised to learn that their new friend is a Christian. But upending their assumptions about Christians is part of what builds trust. Their unexamined perception of Christians weakens as they get to know and like you.

It is important to know that someone who has crossed the threshold from distrust to trust is still far off from a profession of faith. Instead, they have, on a very basic level, decided not to write off Christians entirely. Sure, most Christians are judgmental, they may still think; but you're great. **You're a Christian, and they trust you.**

It's a huge step.

Curiosity

Your new friend may trust you, but they're content to let you keep your "holy religion thing" to yourself—until they wonder what that black smudge on your forehead is one Wednesday in spring.

As your friendship and trust deepen, your friend might become curious about your faith and even curious about Jesus. But hold the phone—they're just curious, not interested! Curiosity is a natural part of friendship and does not yet suggest that the unbeliever is interested in following Jesus or becoming Catholic.

Andrea

When I roomed with two Chinese women during college, I had lots of questions about their heritage and traditions. I also wanted to know about my roommates' interest in health care policy. Likewise, they asked me many questions about my family and upbringing and about my Catholic faith. They knew I spent a lot of time at the Catholic center and wondered what I did there and why it was important to me. In asking these questions, they weren't considering converting; they were just being good friends. They cared about me and my interests.

Even though a curious person isn't interested in your beliefs or practices for themselves, their questions do offer an opportunity to share your faith. The key in this stage is to respond to the questions people are actually asking. If they ask, "Why do you go to church?" tell them, but don't ask if they want to go to church too. Give them your perspective, and share what the practice or belief in question brings to *your* life. Inspire their curiosity, but let them be curious. If they want to know more, they'll ask more questions! But if you try to make your thing *their* thing, you'll scare them off . . . and their questions will cease.

It is, however, totally fair game to ask them questions in response! Curiosity is an exchange, and you can spark their questioning by asking things like "What's your take on the God question?" or "What do you think life is all about?"

Answer your friend's questions as they come, ask them what they believe in return, and pray hard.

Openness

A curious person wants to know about you, but they're not yet open to change. While a curious person is not interested in Jesus or Christianity for themselves, an open person is considering the possibility that Christians may have something they want.

As someone approaches openness, the questions go underground. Instead of asking forthright questions about what you believe, a person begins to ask *themselves* questions, such as, "What do *I* believe?" "If it's no big deal to sleep around, what is that pang I sometimes feel in my gut the next morning?" "Is 'work hard, party hard' all that's in my future?" "Am I the sort of person I hoped I'd be?"

Facing these questions is hard, heroic even. Most people are used to ignoring or suppressing these existential questions when they arise. Crossing from curiosity to openness is one of the hardest thresholds to move through, since it requires your friend to acknowledge a lack, or deficiency, in their own beliefs about the world. It's unsettling. And it takes time.

You can help them in this stage by sharing honestly about your own existential questions and how God enters your own internal conversations. "I get so mad at myself when I nag my husband, *again*. Can't I be better than that? I really try to be loving, but I honestly feel like some days I can't hold my tongue. I've been asking for the grace to change, though, and some days I pause just long enough to rephrase my thought. Do you ever struggle with that?" Sharing in this way and asking your friend if they relate can help the questions continue to percolate.

People in openness may vacillate back and forth between wanting to move forward and jumping back to curiosity.

Walking with someone in openness takes all our patience and prayers.

Continue to lead them and help them imagine themselves as a Christian, but don't pressure them to make a decision. What your friend needs most is space to explore the idea of following Jesus. They need you to walk with them as they try faith on for themselves. They're not committed, but they're tentatively considering what it would be like if they believed what you believe.

Seeking

If the stage of openness is passive and tentative, seeking is active and intentional. At some point, a person on their way to discipleship needs to decide if this "Jesus thing" is for them.

Having come to trust a Christian, to ask their curious questions about Christianity and Jesus, and to consider if Christians have something their life is lacking, the seeker now energetically pursues clarity. "When someone is truly seeking, there is an urgency and purpose to their searching. They feel almost as if it is a quest they are on, and they lean into it with a rather determined posture. Even *they* feel that the time is ripe: they want answers to their questions, they want to come to some conclusions."[54]

It is characteristic of seekers to be seeking *Jesus* rather than "God generally" or vague spiritual experiences. They want to know: "Is Jesus the One I'm looking for?" "Will Jesus answer the questions of my heart?" In their pursuit of answers, they will usually spend plenty of time with Christians, often joining a small group or attending parish events. In contrast with the theoretical considerations of the openness stage, seekers will concretely apply Christian morality to their lifestyle and ask themselves, "Am I ready to give this up? Am I ready for my life to change? Is it worth it?" They recognize that if the answer to their quest results in becoming a Christian, that decision will have consequences. Part of their search involves deciding if they want to take on those consequences.

Seekers are often confused for committed disciples in most parishes and campus ministries. We tend to assume that if people are enthusiastically attending every offering the parish offers up, they are already committed to following Jesus. In fact, they may be enthusiastically *seeking Jesus*, but have not made a decision to be one of his disciples just yet.

You can help a seeker friend when the time is right by prompting them to make that decision and to make an act of faith.

Profession of Faith

The stages preceding discipleship help us articulate people's experience as they begin to discover, desire, and seek Jesus, but it is not enough to seek Jesus. Disciples choose to lay down their lives and follow him.

If, at the culmination of their quest, your friend makes a decision to follow Jesus, a whole new world is opened to them. Their search may be at an end, but their journey is just beginning. One church document says that "such searching, guided by the Holy Spirit and the proclamation of the *Kerygma*, prepares the way for conversion which is certainly 'initial,' but brings with it adherence to Christ and the will to walk in his footsteps."[55]

This "initial" conversion gives new believers the grace and commitment to follow Christ. It ushers them into a period of apprenticeship in the whole Christian life[56] where they desire to know Jesus more deeply and to become more like him by a changed life. They experience all the joys and challenges of life as a disciple.

New or newly awakened believers learn from other Christians how to follow Jesus: in prayer, service, reception of the sacraments, reading of the Scriptures, loving others, and renouncing sin. Christian discipleship is so much more than an intellectual assent. For your friend's act of faith to be fruitful, it must incorporate the intellect, will, and every aspect of their life.

In this period of discipleship, someone who has put their faith in Jesus begins to live out that decision by learning from more experienced Christians. Throughout Nextstep, we have proposed ourselves as your guide in the life of discipleship. Most of the resources you find here aim at apprenticing our readers in the Christian life. As your friend begins to follow Jesus, you can share what you've learned with them here to help guide them along the path.

Importantly, at this point, you don't need to guide your friend on your own. Continue to walk with them, but at this point, your friend is a disciple, and they need the community of disciples (the Church) to guide them as well. Depending on their unique situation, your friend's next step may include preparing for sacraments of initiation to enter the Church. Or they may look to the Sacrament of Reconciliation (sometimes called the "Sacrament of Conversion") to "rid [themselves] of every burden and sin that clings" so that they can "perse-vere in running the race that lies before [them] while keeping [their] eyes fixed on Jesus, the leader and perfecter of faith" (Hebrews 12:1-2, NABRE).

Journey toward Perfection

The final stage the Church lays out for the process of continu-ing conversion is called the "journey toward perfection."[57] Not leaving any of the previous stages behind, but building on them, the person who has a firmly-established life of disci-pleship continues to grow more deeply aligned with God's will and Jesus' call in their life through periods of trial and growth in sacrificial love. Prayer and service deepen. Renunciation of self and reliance on Christ take further root. The "end" of this stage is full union with God—a future only heaven can contain!

As your friend matures, you and they will both rely on the community of the Church for teaching, formation, and exam-ples of others' holiness. In particular, "the Gospel and the Eucharist are the constant food for the journey to the Father's House. The action of the Holy Spirit operates so that the gift of 'communion' and the task of 'mission' are deepened and lived in an increasingly intense way."[58]

The Holy Spirit sweeps us up into the life of God and of the Church (communion), purifying and strengthening our discipleship and holiness. As the fire of God's love and mercy burns more intensely within us, we overflow in a life of mission—lovingly sharing the gospel with others through our words and actions. Our commitment to mission moves us out of our comfort zones, forcing us to rely not on our own strength but on the Lord. Holiness and mission are thus completely united. As we grow in one, we increase in the other.

Disciples need each other, and even disciples journeying toward perfection need each other. We strengthen and guide one another, offering fraternal correction and encouragement. As the author of the Letter to the Hebrews put it, "Let us hold fast the confession of our hope without wavering, for he who promised is faithful; and let us consider how to stir up one another to love and good works, not neglecting to meet together, . . . but encouraging one another" (10:23-25). Hold fast to your hope of full heavenly communion with God. Keep following Jesus. Continue walking with your friend now, not so much as a guide, but as a fellow companion on the road.

Action Step: Make a List

> Every human being is the object of God's infinite tenderness, and he himself is present in their lives. . . . Appearances notwithstanding, every person is immensely holy and deserves our love. . . . It is a wonderful thing to be God's faithful people. We achieve fulfillment when we break down walls and our heart is filled with faces and names! (Pope Francis, *Evangelii Gaudium,* 274)

Take a moment now to call to mind each of the stages:

1. Trust
2. Curiosity
3. Openness
4. Seeking
5. Profession of Faith
6. Journey toward Perfection

As you reflected on the stages, did you think of various people in your life in each stage? Make a list of those people.

With particular names and faces in mind, review the stages, and think of one thing you could do to love, support, and guide your friends according to the stages they are in.

No matter what stages your friends are in, take these names and faces to prayer. The Holy Spirit is the only One who converts hearts. We do our part, but the Lord woos his beloved to give their hearts to him.

Pray for your friends to open themselves to further conversion and for any needs they have.

11

Making Disciples: A Lost Art

This call to make disciples is for all followers
of Jesus to live out. Through genuine,
trusting relationships, each layperson has
the ability to influence a few others.

Sue's Story

Sue had a powerful experience at a weekend retreat. For the
first time in her life, she encountered Christ. He became real
in her heart, knew her by name, and called her to come closer
still. The Mass came alive as never before. She enthusiastically
participated, wanting to pray with her whole heart. She longed
to open herself to Jesus and make him the center of her life.

When Sue returned home, she tried to find anyone she could
talk to about her experience and newly discovered faith. But
Sue couldn't make any connections. Her parish pastoral lead-
ers weren't even sure what she wanted. They did not know
anyone who could apprentice another as a Catholic disciple.

Within a few weeks, the fire that burned so brightly dwin-
dled. Sue felt discouraged. She doubted her own experience.

Sue knew she should probably pray, but she lacked all the support the retreat had provided.

While Sue in this story is fictional, her story—unfortunately—is representative of far too many true stories.

The Need for One-on-One Mentoring in Discipleship

Sue underwent interior conversion to Jesus Christ. What did Sue need after this encounter? What happened to her instead? See her story in the parable of the sower:

> And he taught them many things in parables, and in his teaching he said to them: "Listen! A sower went out to sow. And as he sowed, some seed fell along the path, and the birds came and devoured it. Other seed fell on rocky ground, where it had not much soil, and immediately it sprang up, since it had no depth of soil; and when the sun rose it was scorched, and since it had no root it withered away. . . .
>
> The sower sows the word. And these are the ones along the path, where the word is sown; when they hear, Satan immediately comes and takes away the word which is sown in them. And these in like manner are the ones sown upon rocky ground, who, when they hear the word, immediately receive it with joy; and they have no root in themselves, but endure for a while. (Mark 4:2-6, 14-17)

Sue received the good news with joy, but it had no way to take root because the soil of her spiritual life was shallow. She needed someone who could help her pray, receive the sacraments fruitfully, and read Scripture, seeking God's word for her life. She didn't even know enough to ask for these things. Instead, she remained "harassed and helpless, like sheep without a shepherd" (Matthew 9:36). She was a believer but did not know the way of discipleship—the way of Jesus.

Jesus knew the solution: "The harvest is plentiful, but the laborers are few; pray therefore the Lord of the harvest to send out laborers into his harvest" (Matthew 9:37-38). Sue needed a laborer—a laborer who knew the Lord, knew Sue, and could guide Sue, step-by-step, deeper into the life of discipleship. A laborer who lived out the Great Commission of Jesus to "go . . . and make disciples of all nations" (28:19).

The Church calls this apprenticeship in a life of discipleship "initiatory catechesis."[59] It follows "missionary proclamation" and is an absolutely necessary step in the whole process of evangelization and faith formation.

> The "moment" of catechesis is that which corresponds to the period in which conversion to Jesus Christ is formalized, and provides a basis for first adhering to him. Converts, by means of "a period of formation, an apprenticeship in the whole Christian life," are initiated into the mystery of salvation and an evangelical style of life. This means "initiating the hearers into the fullness of Christian life."[60]

The U. S. Bishops specifically recommend apprenticeship as the ideal means to accomplish this critical stage of evangelization. In "Disciples Called to Witness," they quote from the *National Directory for Catechesis*:

To create a culture of witness, we must live explicit lives of discipleship. Being a disciple is a challenge. Fortunately, one does not become a disciple of Christ on his or her own initiative. The work of the Holy Spirit within the Christian community forms the person as a disciple of Christ. One seeking to learn how to be a disciple of Christ does so through apprenticeship. Those seeking to return to the faith are seeking to live a life of discipleship, to follow in the footsteps of Christ. The parish must provide formed disciples who can accompany those who are returning to the Church and guide them throughout their journey.

Apprenticeship "links an experienced Christian believer, or mentor, with one who seeks a deeper relationship with Christ and the Church." Furthermore, this relationship is a "guided encounter with the entire Christian life, a journey toward conversion to Christ. It is a school for discipleship that promotes an authentic following of Christ based on the acceptance of one's baptismal responsibilities, the internalization of the word of God, and the transformation of the whole person to 'life in Christ.'" Apprenticeship is an essential element in witnessing to the Gospel message."[61]

Initiatory Catechesis Is Crucial

The Church distinguishes initiatory catechesis from "perfective" (sometimes called "permanent") (*General Directory for Catechesis*, 71) catechesis in that "being essential, it looks to what is 'common' for the Christian, without entering into disputed questions nor transforming itself into a form of theological investigation" (68).

Anyone young in the Christian life and hungry for God needs this special period of apprenticeship in the heart and habits of discipleship (daily prayer, a rich sacramental life, devotion to Scripture, intentional community, the basics of understanding and living out the vocation of the laity, etc.). And this need goes far beyond those being initiated into the Church. Many Catholics who have received all three sacraments of initiation have not yet been awakened personally and spiritually to the heart and habits of discipleship. They may attend Sunday Mass regularly (or somewhat regularly), but many are far from the Sacrament of Reconciliation, do not strive to spend focused quiet time each day for mental prayer and Scripture meditation, and are rarely if ever accompanied personally in practical matters of faith pertaining to their state in life.

Unfortunately, outside of youth programs and RCIA, it is hard to find help for spiritually hungry believers like Sue. Many communities try to organize programs and offer events aiming to feed and form those like Sue, but classically. only the same twenty to a hundred parishioners show up to program after program and event after event. Many more would soak up the heart and habits of discipleship if this lifestyle were not only the subject of catechetical parish offerings but were the lifeblood of intentional friendships formed by a growing number of lay missionary disciples in a community. As it stands, most catechetical program attenders do not receive the needed apostolic formation to go out and find, walk with, pray for, and apprentice those like Sue, who, for whatever reason, might not be showing up to those catechetical programs.

Who will be the personal spiritual friend who can inspire, guide, and assist the hungry believers in discovering and growing in the way of Jesus?

Without developing a spiritual friendship in which they can find personal guidance and support, people like Sue often either fall back into their pre-conversion lifestyle or become volunteers for their parish or campus ministry. Sue could have visited many ministries and seen that "involvement" is what a committed Catholic does. That could mean dishing up donuts on Sundays after Mass, serving the poor, or joining the finance council. The parish would have another hand on deck, helping with good initiatives, but Sue would not have received the formation the Church says she needs. She will not have become a disciple who is on her way to making other disciples.

Tasks need doing, and service to the poor is always an essential part of discipleship, but those lacking the heart and habits of a disciple must not be deprived of the formation they need to grow and mature as Catholics.

Just as Jesus saw the desperate need for shepherds who could guide and care for his sheep, the Church recognizes that initiatory catechesis is necessary and crucial.

Initiatory catechesis is thus the necessary link between missionary activity which calls to faith and pastoral activity which continually nourishes the Christian community. This is not, therefore, an optional activity, but basic and fundamental for building up the personality of the individual disciple, as it is for the whole Christian community. Without it, missionary activity lacks continuity and is sterile, while pastoral activity lacks roots and becomes superficial and confused: any misfortune could cause the collapse of the entire building.[62]

To be "sterile" means to bear no fruit for the kingdom. In this age of declining Mass attendance, the Church desperately needs spiritually fruitful laborers. We see too often a collapse of faith among those for whom Jesus never truly became Savior, brother, and friend.

The Laborers Are Few

In this age, the Church needs lay missionary disciples who can guide, accompany, and apprentice just a few individuals with whom they have trusting relationships. We must respond now to the Great Commission of Jesus to go and make disciples!

This call to make disciples is for all followers of Jesus to live out. Through genuine, trusting relationships, each layperson has the ability to influence a few others.

A Broad Definition of "One-on-Ones"

The following chapter offers a few tools and tips for making disciples. Before moving on to those, let us summarize what has been said and clarify how we will use the shorthand term "one-on-ones" going forward.

By speaking broadly of "one-on-ones," we mean: guiding and accompanying individuals into deeper friendship with Jesus.

"One-on-one" describes the context for conversation better than the content of it. As disciples deeply connect with Christ and hone their skills for loving relationships, they will undoubtedly build friendships with people on a broad spectrum. Some may distrust faith of any kind, while others may firmly hold faith in Jesus Christ and his Church. One-on-one conversation is invaluable at any point along this road, but it takes on different characteristics depending on the spiritual maturity of the participants.

In the Great Commission, Jesus instructs us,

> Go . . . and make disciples of all nations, baptizing them in the name of the Father, and of the Son and of the Holy Spirit, teaching them to observe all that I have commanded you. (Matthew 28:19-20)

How do we "go . . . and make disciples"? In many ways, of course. Making disciples is a shared effort of the whole Church, and there are many settings in which the Great Commission must be lived out. The family is the basic setting to begin forming disciples of Jesus. The sacraments provide an essential foundation and nourishment in the life of discipleship. Parish communities, schools, ministry programs, books, movies, and online resources can all help in the formation of disciples, especially with regard to "teaching them to observe all that I have commanded you."

Underlying all of the above is a simple and important truth: *disciples play active roles in forming other disciples through intentional relationships, personalized care, intercessory prayer, and spiritual guidance.*

We use the phrases "one-on-one" and "person to person" to emphasize and call forth this active, personal role that each layperson is called to play in the lives of at least a few others.

Jesus chose a handful of people to invest in deeply, spending even more time with Peter, James, and John than he did with the rest of the Twelve. Just so, baptized and confirmed disciples of Jesus invest relationally in the lives of a few others to help them mature and bear good fruit in the kingdom.

For parents this mission includes their children, of course, but the call to make disciples—even for parents—goes beyond the raising of their children. And as most parents will agree, they often need other disciple makers from outside the family to inspire and mentor their children at any stage of their development, often well into adulthood.

The fact remains that many adults, young and old, are believers in God but do not follow Jesus intimately as friend and Lord. They do not know the voice of the Good Shepherd, who calls them to follow him more closely, that he might lead them into greener pastures.

Who will inspire and win the trust of these people?

Who will spark their curiosity and whet their appetite for more truth, goodness, and beauty?

Who will show them the way of Jesus?

It could be you.

I Am Not a Runner

Andre

"I am not a runner."

That's what I told myself and others for over twenty years. This probably has to do with the fact that I ran four miles once while in high school and became sick with mono the next day. Whether consciously or subconsciously, I don't remember, but somewhere inside my mind I drew a conclusion that day: "I am not a runner."

While I remained fairly physically active over the next twenty years (raising four kids tends to do that for a person), I was never one to establish any kind of intentional exercise routine or habits. I had a vague sense that as I headed towards my forties that *I should probably establish some kind of habit of getting my heart rate up regularly.* At times I found myself wishing I were one of "those people" who actually *liked* running or some other discipline of exercise. One summer I even made a plan to run or bike four days a week. It lasted two weeks. I simply was *not* one of "those people" who liked to exercise! Who was I kidding anyways? After all, I had known for the last twenty years that "I'm not a runner."

A few years later, I started experiencing some heightened anxiety through a number of challenging new situations in my life. I would pray and keep afloat by grace, the sacraments, hard work, a few friends, a spiritual director and, for a time, the help of a wonderful therapist, but I knew there was something missing from my holistic picture of mental, spiritual, and physical health: exercise. I believed all the science about the effects of exercise not only on the body but also on the mind, and more than ever before, I desired to be someone who exercised.

Around this time I went on a vacation with my friend Michael, who lived about three hours away. Both of our families (eight kids, twelve people in all) piled into a single RV and headed west for an incredible week of adventure, exploring national parks and breathtaking views.

As Michael and I shared some quality talk time in the front seats of the RV, he learned about my recent struggles with anxiety and of my desire to finally do some running or regular exercise. It turns out Michael had recently gotten into running. After talking for a while, Michael asked me, "Want to go for a run tomorrow morning? Let's go together."

"Yes I do," I told him. I warned him he might need to go a bit slower (or a lot slower!) than he was used to, but he didn't mind. The next morning, we ran three miles through the Black Hills of South Dakota. We chatted along much of the way, continuing to share our joys and sorrows with each other. At the end of this run, Michael asked me if he could lead us in prayer. I gladly consented; he closed our run by thanking the Lord for our friendship and this beautiful scenery. He lifted up my sorrows and anxieties to the Lord in this prayer, along with whatever else we had discussed along the way. As we got back to the RV, our wives and kids were just starting to awaken for another day of adventure.

It was one of the most positive experiences of running I had ever had because I did it with a friend. It also helped me realize that I could actually do this (run). It wasn't the scary and intimidating prospect I thought it might be. I was convinced more than ever that I wanted—and needed—to exercise.

A few weeks after our trip, Michael texted, "Andre, you should run a half marathon next year. You're ready for this, and I think you'll love it! Pick a race, send me the date, and I'll come and run it with you. What do you think?"

At first, I chuckled at the thought, *Yeah right. I'm still not a runner.* But the idea sank in, and by the time I texted him back, I was pretty sure I wanted to do it. A month later I was certain I wanted to do it. Another month later I had registered for a half marathon ten months away and had even gotten three other guys to agree to do it with me. I knew that if I was going to do this, I would need the support of a training buddy or two.

Though I didn't see Michael during the training process, we would talk or text on occasion to keep in touch. In addition to catching up on life, he would ask about how my running was coming. I would often ask him a question about some running gear or strategies.

The race itself was an incredible experience. The excitement of race day, the strength we found deep within ourselves, and the companionship of one another amounted to an energy and a determination that took us by surprise. We were shocked when our scores showed a pace of over a minute per mile faster than any of our training runs.

Michael celebrated with me. I thanked him for inspiring me by his example, listening to me in my struggles, taking those early steps with me by running together, praying for me, challenging me when the time was right, and offering me his unfailing accompaniment and guidance throughout it all.

Run so as to win.
—1 Corinthians 9:24, NABRE

What would it look like if there were more "Michaels" in our world—not just with regard to running, but also on the path of discipleship?

What if, when a friend of yours opens up to you about struggles they are facing or expresses vague desires to "pray better" or to "learn more about their faith," you responded with just the right kind of love, care, and guidance to meet them where they are and help them take the next step?

What if, on the path of life, each disciple of Jesus Christ discerned, invited, and apprenticed one or a few others into a more mature and fruitful life of following Jesus?

What if pastors did not need to attempt to launch every catechetical program they could find and beg for volunteers and attendees, because so many of their parishioners were busy, of their own initiative, helping a few others learn the ways of Jesus?

We created the *Nextstep* books—along with the online material found at www.ecnextstep.com—to help individuals take their next steps in faith and to equip those laborers seeking to make disciples with a resource to journey through with others.

Now that you're in Part 4 ("Become a Guide"), you can look back upon the three previous parts with a view towards individuals in your life who might be ready for a more serious commitment or a more direct challenge to grow in the fundamentals of discipleship (initiatory catechesis).

Part 1 (in Volume 1) seeks to (re)establish a firm foundation of faith in the essential proclamation—the good news of

God's love revealed in Jesus Christ and brought to us in word and sacrament through the ministry of the Church.

Part 2 (in Volume 1) is a suggested path through the fundamental, transformative habits of prayer, Scripture, Eucharist, Reconciliation, and community.

Part 3 (in this volume) digs deeper into discipleship topics and habits, including growth in virtue, sharing good news in word and deed, and maturing through challenges with a deeper embrace of prayer, Scripture, sacraments and community.

- **Is there someone in your life, expressing to you (directly or indirectly) a desire to grow? Could you be the friend and guide they need to help them take the next step in following Jesus?**

The next (and final) chapter presents some methods and tools to help you keep asking this question, and to move forward in living out the Great Commission when the answer is yes.

12

Suggestions for Making Disciples

The Lord is preparing people to grow in him as a result of your prayer and friendship.

By the Grace of God

> *And the word of God increased; and the number of the disciples multiplied greatly.*
> —Acts 6:7

With utmost reverence for both the challenges and the variety of ways to foster growth in others, we offer here a few considerations that we pray might be of some use to our readers who seek to make disciples. Keep in mind, of course, that "unless the LORD builds the house, / those who build it labor in vain" (Psalm 127:1). No technique, formula, or tool will in itself be fruitful for making disciples. The mystery of God, of grace, and of each unique person must be approached with all reverence and humility. And we must seek the Holy Spirit to guide us, who alone is "the principal agent of evangelization."[63] May these words that follow serve to help us labor well in vineyard of the Lord.

Whom to Invite

Recall the common stages of conversion discussed in chapter 10: trust, curiosity, openness, seeking, faith, and journey towards perfection. In this section, we want to focus on those individuals in our lives who are seeking to grow in faith and discipleship. Recall the story of Sue from the beginning of chapter 11. She had a recent awakening of faith and wanted to grow in understanding Scripture, prayer, and her vocation better. But your own examples might look quite different. The Lord is preparing people to grow in him as a result of your prayer and friendship.

Consider these questions as you think and pray over the people in your life:

- **Who has asked you questions about faith or meaningful topics?**

- **Who has expressed to you some kind of hunger to grow or change?**

- **Have you had deeper conversations about faith with someone, but busyness got in the way of following up or pursuing more intentional growth together?**

- With whom do you think you could grow into a better Christian friendship through a mutual sharing of faith?

Get to Know Their Stories of Faith

As you think of people who have shared with you some measure of their hunger for spiritual growth, ask yourself how well you know their stories of faith. Have they already shared significant parts of it with you? If not, you might want to start with an initial goal of getting to know them better and hearing more about their faith stories. How might you ask about this in a natural way?

Think about a way you could invite someone to get together in a way that is fitting for your life. Perhaps you could get together for coffee or a meal or go for a jog together. Perhaps you will get the chance to chat at a social event or at a kid's soccer game. Whatever and wherever your opportunity to chat may be, consider the following options for drawing out someone's faith story:

- Ask easy-to-answer questions at whatever depth will be comfortable for them. Possible examples: "Have you always gone to Mass?" "Did you grow up Catholic?" "Was your family religious growing up?"

- Or follow up on something they shared previously: "I remember you said something about a mission trip that made an impact on you. Where did you go?" Seek meaningful details if the person responds without any: "How did that affect your faith?"

- Ask a question that might help transition from life to faith, for someone who is already comfortable talking about God, such as "Where is/was God for you in that?" (referring to a story or situation the person just shared).

- Share some of your own faith story or something that reveals a bit of who you are, if it's natural. Do your best to be reciprocal in the conversation without allowing your stories to dominate.

- Do not give unsolicited advice.

Inviting Someone to Meet Regularly (for a Time)

As you grow in the habit of strengthening friendships and discovering more about peoples' faith experiences through natural conversation, there likely will come a time when someone's hunger to grow is evident. Perhaps a conversation in which you shared faith stories was particularly easy and mutually enriching, or perhaps the person directly expressed to you a desire to grow in prayer or in faith. It could also be a less "spiritual" topic about which the person opened up to you: a desire to be a better parent or spouse, for example, or the need for guidance on making an important decision.

In any case, one way to help you discern someone's level of experience in discipleship or interest in growing is simply by asking something like, "Do you have any kind of daily prayer habit or routine?"

If they say yes, this could open up fruitful sharing from both of you in conversation.

If they say no, or if they indicate a desire to grow in this area, ask a follow-up question: "Would you want some help developing one?" Remember, you're not having this conversation with a stranger, but with a friend who has already shared with you some of their faith journey and at least a bit of their desire to grow.

If they say yes to wanting some help developing a stronger prayer life, propose meeting weekly or every other week for an initial four times or so. This will give you a good chance to cover some ground in your subsequent conversations, without it sounding like an overwhelming commitment. Asking about a prayer routine is an effective doorway into many further discussion topics relating to a life of discipleship. Prayer is central to all aspects of our lives, and people often desire to experience more in prayer. They just don't know how.

Is the Lord opening a door to further conversation about discipleship with someone he has placed in your life? If so, pray about what way will be most natural for you to invite this person to chat once or through an initial series of get-togethers over a number of weeks.

Deciding what to do after an initial three or four meetings won't be difficult. If the meetings are mutually enjoyable and seem spiritually fruitful, keep going for another month or two if you're able. Seek to establish them as effectively as you can in the core habits and attitudes of discipleship represented in *Nextstep*, Volumes 1 and 2 (Parts 1-3), which walk through various topics in the Discipleship Wheel, found in appendix A in this book. See also www.ecnextstep.com for more content and tools for guiding others in their next steps.

No two people's journeys are exactly alike, nor can we predict just what each person needs or how accompanying and apprenticing them will go. We simply seek to follow the Lord through every door he opens for us to help another person take their next step in the ways of Jesus.

A General Structure for Regular One-on-Ones

Recall that the goal of meeting one-on-one with someone regularly for a time is to guide, inspire, and accompany them, step-by-step, into a deeper following of Jesus. In other words, it's to help them take the next step in discipleship. By following Jesus more attentively, they will experience the greater freedom that Jesus longs to give them.

As you gain opportunities to meet with some individuals regularly and repeatedly, the three words—"life," "growth," and "mission"—may provide a helpful structure in preparing for and facilitating discipleship conversations.

Life

Person-to-person relationships require getting to know each other on the level of regular day-to-day events and interests. One-on-ones can and should be fun and lighthearted in addition to being important and meaningful.

Ask how they are doing. Follow up on something they told you last time.

- "How was your vacation?"

- "How is Janet's job search going?"

- "Any updates on your mother's health?"

Briefly share something from your own life too.

Growth

No matter the current spiritual maturity of the person you're meeting one-on-one, you can be intentional about their growth. Meet them where they are, and help them take the next step. Prepare content on an aspect of discipleship that the person desires to strengthen, or guide them systematically through the contents of *Nextstep*.

Decide ahead of time what topic you will plan to discuss and how you will do it. It's okay to diverge from your plan as the situation demands or the Holy Spirit leads, but coming prepared with a plan is key.

Follow up on any previous commitments to prayer or spiritual practices.

- Was there an action, prayer, or reading plan from last time you met that you can follow up on?

- If they are praying regularly, you could ask, "What stood out to you in prayer since we last met?"

- Offer encouragement and support as they share any obstacles they encountered in prayer or other spiritual practices.

Lead a conversation that explores the topic. Introduce the discipleship topic, and ask about their experience.

Utilize Scripture, personal experience, and thoughtful questions as your primary resources for dialogical teaching. As a general rule, aim to open the Bible together frequently. Encourage them to bring their own Bible to your meetings.

Plan a few easy-to-ask questions that will help you engage the person with this topic.

In the course of the conversation, share some of your own experiences and answer questions they have if you're able. If they ask a question you can't answer, simply say you don't know. If it's an important matter to the person and there is an answer in the Catholic Tradition that would bring helpful clarity, you may wish to explore it together or do some research and get back to them.

Mission

Growth in discipleship necessarily spills outward into life, application, and mission. Prompt them to consider what the next steps are to growing both interiorly and outwardly. In other words,

- How can they grow interiorly in their life with Christ as a result of this conversation?

- How are they growing outwardly to love, serve, and pray for others?

The following are some specific prompts and options that may help you guide them in their next steps:

- Encourage them to commit to a regular prayer habit.

- Guide them to engage in discipleship practices in their daily life.

- What's one concrete step they can take to strengthen discipleship habits based on your discussion? Involve them in this, but also propose steps and offer guidance.

Also, you could ask something like "Who will experience God's love through you this week? How?" In other words, whom are they called to pray for and intentionally love/serve right now? What does that look like? How is that going?

For married people, it's good for them to think of their spouse when first considering this question, and you might help them to do this. It can also be a friend, a son or daughter, a coworker, a neighbor, or some other acquaintance who is hurting or has opened up to them recently. Don't force them to choose someone every time you meet, but regularly asking questions like these encourages the habit of reflecting on specific ways the Lord is calling them to be good news to others. It also helps you to know them better and to pray for them more specifically.

Consider asking:

- "How can I pray for you?"

- "Is there anything you want help with or accountability on?"

Schedule or confirm the next meeting (ideally in one or two weeks).

Prayer Together

Praying aloud, one-on-one, is a not only fruitful because of the power of prayer, but it's also incredibly formative for faith and discipleship. By praying aloud for and with someone in your own words, you model an intimate and conversational relationship with God. You provide guidance by example and inspiration for how the other person might learn to talk to God in their private prayer times as well when they are with others.

When you get the chance to guide and accompany someone in their walk of discipleship for a time, start and end your meetings together with prayer. Here are a few suggestions:

- **Pray briefly in your own words to begin a one-on-one (either right at the start, or as a transition from the "life" to the "growth" portion of the conversation). Share the task of leading the prayer as each is comfortable.**

- **After discussing life, growth, and mission, bring the themes of your conversation and any life circumstances discussed** to the Lord in prayer. Encourage their participation in this prayer as they feel comfortable. For example, "Let's wrap up in prayer. How about I open and you close our prayer?"

See more on praying aloud for and with others in the section coming up on leading extemporaneous prayer.

After Your Meeting

Write down some notes on your conversation. This will help you remember what was said and help you pray for them. Add their prayer requests to your prayer intentions list. Pray for them regularly and for how God wants to use you in their life.

Stay in touch as much as is helpful and natural between meetings (such as a brief encouraging text, email, or phone call, etc.).

Leading Extemporaneous Prayer: An Essential Skill

By "extemporaneous prayer," we mean praying aloud in your own words and seeking the Holy Spirit's guidance for how to pray.

By leading another person in extemporaneous prayer, you set the tone and model the heart of a disciple and disciplemaker.

While you may wish to use a few prayers of the Church here and there, we recommend that the default method of prayer with and for others be extemporaneous prayer. You're forming people to seek and respond to the promptings of the Holy Spirit. That requires talking and listening to God.

Peter Kreeft, noted Catholic scholar and author, explains the necessity of using our own words in prayer and teaching others to do so:

> When we use the prayers of the Church, we use the greatest prayers ever written, the words and sentiments of great saints and hymn writers and liturgists. We do this rightly, because God deserves the best, and these prayers are the best. They were composed by other people, but we make them our own when we pray them, like a lover reciting a sonnet by Shakespeare to his beloved. . . .
>
> But if others' words are the *only* words lovers use to each other, they are not lovers but performers. We must not only "say our prayers," we must pray. Others' words may be more beautiful, but your words are more yours, and God cherishes them as a father cherishes his child's own crude drawing made just for him more than he cherishes the greatest work of art in the world. God wants your own words most of all because they are your own; they come from your heart, and your heart is what your Lover craves.[64]

As Kreeft notes, eloquence is not the point. Many people fear praying aloud because they fear they will stumble over their words or sound less than profound. Yet we do a great disservice to others and to ourselves if we only deliver eloquent speeches to the Lord in prayer. Humans stumble over their words all the time in regular, daily conversation. Friends don't wait to have all their thoughts ironed out or rehearsed before opening their mouths in conversation. So too, let us not be afraid to model for others what it can look like to talk to

God simply and directly, as friends, as a child to a Father. This practice alone can do wonders for a person's spiritual growth and intimacy with the Lord.

How to Pray Extemporaneously: Some Tips

Above all, pray from the heart, in your own words.

Address the Lord directly; speak to God rather than about God. Don't say, "I'd like to pray that God blesses . . ." but, rather, "Lord, please bless our time together." Speak in your own natural voice, not a "churchy" voice.

Speak to the Persons of our triune God rather than to "God" generically. Address your prayer to a Person of the Trinity: the Father, Jesus, or the Holy Spirit. We all need to grow in our relationship with all three Persons of the Trinity. Directing prayer to a specific Person of the Trinity can help.

Model your personal relationship with Jesus. Show your trust in him. Let your prayer demonstrate how you turn to Jesus with your own challenges. Exhibit the burning love of the Savior for people you pray for.

Praise God in your own words. Practice on your own. Grow in ease by first using some praises from the psalms. Make the words of a psalm your own. Alter the language, and use your own vocabulary and style as much as possible.

Intercede with confidence: for your friend, for people you both know, for the Church, and for the greater community. Pray for the person you're meeting with and for people in both of your lives that may come up in your discussions. Remember that, mysterious as it is, intercessory prayer is not just something we do to remind ourselves about the plight of people we love; we believe it actually matters and bears fruit!

Intercessory prayers provide space for God to build our spirits for mission, plant words in our hearts, and strengthen our resolve.

How to Pray Extemporaneously: An Outline

Praise God! Say what a great and wonderful God our Father is. Borrow language from the psalms of praise if you don't have your own. For example, see Psalm 8 or Psalm 145.

Thank God! Thank the Lord for the gift of gathering together. Thank him for any blessings the person may have shared about their life. Thank him for the encouragement he gives you both through these conversations together.

Ask God for your needs, the needs of your friend, and anyone whose needs are evident, based on your conversation. Ask God to bless your time together as you begin your chat, to make it fruitful for his kingdom, and to keep you connected to him as you depart.

Close by invoking Jesus: "We pray this through Christ our Lord" or "We pray this in Jesus' name."

You may wish to close by entrusting all these prayers to the care and intercession of Mary by reciting a Hail Mary together. "Mother Mary, we also ask for your protection and intercession for all of the intentions we just shared. Help us to follow your Son in all we do. Hail Mary, full of grace . . ."

End with the Sign of the Cross.

Action Step: Help Someone Take the Next Step

Now do it!

Use the guidelines here in Part 4 of *Nextstep* to help you get started in making disciples—or to bring greater intentionality to an existing spiritual friendship. Through the guidance of the Holy Spirit, pray to know what steps to take with whom.

What's your next step in helping someone else take theirs?

For more guidance on your journey of making disciples, check out www.ecnextstep.com. Find guides for many discipleship topics, practices, and conversations, both for your own growth and to help you guide others.

See also the appendices in this volume, briefly described here:

Appendix A: The Discipleship Wheel

The Evangelical Catholic's outline of discipleship habits and attitudes, inspired by the *General Directory for Catechesis*.

Appendix B: A Discipleship Plan

A goal-setting template for time-honored and transformative Catholic disciplines and practices.

Appendix C: Nine Essentials of a Disciple Maker
A summary of the main characteristics and practices of spiritual guides and mentors. Includes a few questions under each "essential" for self-reflection and examination.

Appendix D: Tips for Motivating Change

An essay containing a number of helpful paradigms and approaches to help you find effective ways to motivate others in your life.

Appendix E: Questions of the Heart

A list of fifty powerful questions for personal use as well as for deepening our spiritual conversations. This appendix includes an introductory essay about the role of questions in our lives and several ways to use this list.

Imagine if it were far more normal for Catholics to regularly gather in pairs to discuss life, growth, and mission together! What would a stronger culture of spiritual accompaniment and one-on-one disciple making look like? We'll never know if we don't ask the Lord to give us his eyes, his ears, and his shepherd's heart for "the one" (or two, or three) in each of our lives whom Jesus calls us to guide along the narrow way.

As iron sharpens iron, / so one person sharpens another.
—Proverbs 27:17, NIV

Appendix A

The Discipleship Wheel

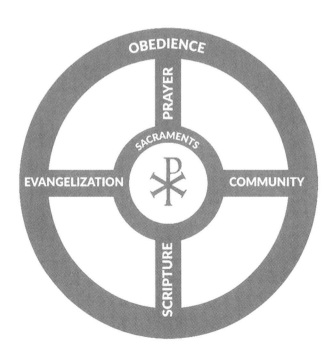

This Discipleship Wheel[65] shows, in a simple way, the basic elements of a life in Christ. If you incorporate each of them into your life of discipleship, your spiritual "wheel" will keep moving you closer to him.

We can use this tool to help us categorize the different habits of a disciple and grow into the ones in which we are weak. The categories provided by the wheel run parallel with instructions on the tasks of initiatory catechesis in the *General Directory for Catechesis*, 84–87.

If we look closely, the wheel actually looks like a monstrance, which is, in a sense, what we become when we live out radiant lives of intentional discipleship. We become transparent; Jesus is held up in and through us for the world to see.

The Hub: Christ the Center

I have been crucified with Christ; it is no longer I who live, but Christ who lives in me; and the life I now live in the flesh I live by faith in the Son of God, who loved me and gave himself for me.
—Galatians 2:20

Christ is the center of all reality, but we must let him become the center of our lives. When we do, our heart finds peace.

Once he has the central position, Jesus sets you on your own journey of becoming like him. You put more and more trust in God, that his ways are the best for you and that he will provide everything you need to live as he wants you to live. You believe this is the only way to happiness.

Inner Rim: Sacramental Life

So those who received his word were baptized. . . . And they
devoted themselves to the apostles' teaching and fellowship,
to the breaking of bread and the prayers.
—Acts 2: 41-42

The sacramental life draws us ever more deeply into the life
of Christ through his body, the Church. If the Church is the
body of Christ, the sacraments most effectively carry the blood
to the members. Thus the sacramental life is drawn in a circle
around Christ, the center of our lives.

When we approach the sacraments with open and prayerful
hearts, we give glory to God and receive the specific gift of that
particular sacrament: in Mass, we partake in the Body and Blood
of Jesus; in Reconciliation, ongoing conversion through the recognition and forgiveness for our sins. The seven sacraments of
the Church are Baptism, Eucharist, Confirmation, Reconciliation, Anointing of the Sick, Matrimony, and Holy Orders.

Vertical Axis

This axis represents our direct relationship with Jesus and the
Father in the Holy Spirit.

Prayer

Have no anxiety about anything, but in everything by prayer and supplication with thanksgiving let your requests be made known to God. And the peace of God, which passes all understanding, will keep your hearts and your minds in Christ Jesus.
—Philippians 4:6-7

Prayer is simply talking with and listening to God as we would a close friend. In prayer, we meet God and experience his love. As followers of Jesus, we pray communally as in our Eucharistic liturgy, but also privately in our inner room.

Daily personal conversational prayer is essential to fostering our relationship with Jesus. The acronym ACTS helps to structure an interior prayer time: Adoration, Contrition, Thanksgiving, Supplication.

Growing in personal prayer helps us to open our hearts more to benefit from the sacramental grace we receive, especially every time we partake of the Eucharist or the Sacrament of Reconciliation.

Scripture

Thy word is a lamp to my feet / and a light to my path.
—Psalm 119:105

God communicates with us in many ways, but primarily through the Scriptures and the Church. When we read and meditate on his word, with the help of the Holy Spirit, we get to know him more and become closer to him. The teachings of the Church help guide us as we grow in this knowledge and assist us to live as Christ taught.

Horizontal Axis

This axis represents our relationships with other people as members of Christ's body.

Community

> *For where two or three are gathered in my name,*
> *there am I in the midst of them.*
> —Matthew 18:20

The Holy Spirit binds followers of Jesus together in love. Jesus did not intend for us to live what he asks of us all on our own. We need one another for support, encouragement, and accountability. Fostering relationships with others who have also made Christ the center of their lives makes possible growth and perseverance in following Jesus. Participation in a small Christian community, Bible study, or prayer group at your church are ways to do this.

For I am not ashamed of the gospel: it is the power
of God for salvation to every one who has faith,
to the Jew first and also to the Greek.
—Romans 1:16

Evangelization is sharing the good news of Jesus Christ with others. The Church exists to bring the gospel of Jesus Christ to the world. When we follow Jesus, we want to share with others the joy, peace, and love we have found in him. It is the natural overflow of his life in us.

We witness to the goodness and power of the gospel by what we say, how we live, and how we love others (see John 13:34-35). These three essential dimensions of evangelization are known as the witness of word, life, and community.

Outer Rim: Obedience to Christ and His Church

He who has my commandments and keeps them, he it is
who loves me; and he who loves me will be loved by my
Father, and I will love him and manifest myself to him.
—John 14:21

Obedience, or living out our relationship with Christ in our attitudes and actions, keeps the Discipleship Wheel all together and mobilizes us for mission. God gives us the Scriptures, the Church, and the Holy Spirit to help us know how best to follow him.

It is not always easy to live in obedience to the commandments, but God promises to enable us to do all things through Jesus Christ in the power of the Holy Spirit (see John 14:25; Philippians 4:13). If you obey him even when it is difficult, he will work it out for your good, as the Scriptures promise (see Romans 8:28). Everything God has asked of us is for one purpose: that our joy may be complete in loving him and in loving one another as Christ loves us.

"All of these tasks are necessary. . . . These tasks are interdependent and develop together" (*General Directory for Catechesis*, 87).

Appendix B

A Discipleship Plan

Prompts for Growing with Jesus

This planning guide presents the transformative practices and disciplines by which we Catholics learn the ways of Jesus and open ourselves to the Holy Spirit. The *Catechism* beautifully summarizes our vocation in Christ Jesus: "We are called only to become one with him, for he enables us as the members of his Body to share in what he lived for us in his flesh as our model" (521).

Use this tool to examine your spiritual practices and to make plans for continued growth in becoming one with Jesus. Do not expect to grow in all of these at once, nor think of this tool as a checklist of external rules. Instead, seek long-term authentic growth in prayer and virtue through various seasons of life.

Be both patient and persistent as you grow into the freedom of the children of God.

Sacramental Life

All the sacraments are sacred links uniting the faithful with one another and binding them to Jesus Christ.
—Catechism, 950

- How often will I go to Mass?

- When/where?

- What practices and prayers (before, during, or after Mass) can help me most fully participate interiorly in the Mass?

- How often will I go to Confession?

- When/where?

- What practices and prayers will help me prepare to make a good confession?

Personal Prayer and Scripture Reading

St. Teresa of Avila said prayer is "frequently conversing in secret with Him Who . . . loves us."[66] Further, the *Catechism* states, "The Church 'forcefully and specifically exhorts all the Christian faithful . . . to learn the surpassing knowledge of Jesus Christ, by frequent reading of the divine Scriptures. 'Ignorance of Scripture is ignorance of Christ'" (133, referencing

Dei Verbum, 25; cf. Philippians 3:8; and and St. Jerome). See resources at www.evangelicalcatholic.org/onepercent.

- **When will I pray and for how long?**

- **Where will I pray?**

- **When/how will I make frequent use of Scripture in my prayer life?**

Spiritual Reading

We benefit greatly from the written wisdom and inspiration found in Catholic Tradition: saints, the *Catechism*, and contemporary authors and teachers.

It tends to work well for people with busy lives to set aside small chunks of time for reading. Even ten to twenty pages a week goes a long way if we're faithful to the practice.

- **I will read [what book?].**

- **By [when?].**

- **Or I will do approximately ____ minutes of spiritual reading each [day/week].**

Devotion to Mary

Mary occupies a special place in the lives of Catholic disciples of Jesus. As Jesus loved his mother, so do we. Mary models a life of submission to God's will, she accompanies us on our journey with her Son, and she intercedes for the world. Saints throughout history have exhibited special devotion to Our Lady, and the Rosary has long been a particularly powerful means of prayer—both for intercession and for meditating upon the life of Christ.

- **How will I honor Mary in prayer during this season of my life?**

Good News to the World

How is the Lord calling you to be good news to others *right now*?

The works of mercy from Scripture and Catholic Tradition are a helpful list for reflecting on this question. Prayerfully read the works of mercy below, and ask the Lord to bring to mind any people he is calling you to serve in one of these ways. Remember, God calls us first to our family and/or to those whom he has placed directly in our lives. Think also of your faith community and of the Lord's special concern for those on the margins. Be careful not to heap up unrealistic intentions. Choose one or two items (perhaps one from each list), and make a simple and concrete plan to live it out in the weeks ahead.

Corporal Works of Mercy

- Feed the hungry.

- Give drink to the thirsty.

- Shelter the homeless.

- Clothe the naked.

- Visit the sick and imprisoned.

- Ransom the captive.

- Bury the dead.

Spiritual Works of Mercy

- Instruct the ignorant.

- Counsel the doubtful.

- Admonish the sinner.

- Bear wrongs patiently.

- Forgive offenses willingly.

- Comfort the afflicted.

- Pray for the living and the dead.

Additional Spiritual Exercises and Devotions

Are there other prayer methods or spiritual exercises that you want in your plan? For example, a daily morning offering, an evening examination, Liturgy of the Hours, the Angelus at noon, other devotions, Scripture memory, fasting, an annual retreat, etc. List any here and indicate the frequency. Once again, be careful not to select too many devotions and practices; you can always add more later.

Share Your Resources

Honor the Lord *. . . / with the first fruits of all your produce.*
—Proverbs 3:9

The clear biblical call to share a portion of our financial resources not only provides for those in need, but it is essential for our growth in discipline and Christian freedom. We also share our time and our talent, but Scripture and Church teaching make it clear we don't share those in lieu of giving financially. What we give remains a private matter to pray about. Percentages give a perspective that sheer dollar amounts do not. Deciding prayerfully what percentage you will give in the upcoming year frees you to detach from that money and more joyfully bless others with it.

- **What percentage of my income will I give away this year?**

- **To the Church? Parish/Diocese?**

- **To charities/causes? Which ones?**

Spiritual Accompaniment

Don't be a "lone ranger" Christian. Get together regularly with at least one person to discuss progress, lessons, insights, and share prayer intentions.

- **With whom will I share some of my goals, progress, and challenges?**

- **When, how often, and where will we get together?**

Additional Tips

Be SMART

SMART goals are Specific, Measurable, Achievable, Relevant, and Time-Bound. "I want to pray more" is not specific, measurable, or time bound, and "I will pray for an hour every morning before my kids wake up" may not be achievable for a parent of young children.

Examples of SMART goals:

- **"I will pray for fifteen minutes a day using the Gospel of the day for three weeks."**

- **"I will go to Mass one more day a week than I currently go, for one month."**

Write down your goals, and tell another person about them. Expect to struggle, and adjust your plan as you go. Always remember that God's love and mercy are not dependent upon our performance! Joyfully persevere in running with Jesus and learning from him. It's a marathon, not a sprint, and we never journey alone.

Call upon Heaven

Say a prayer of commitment to Jesus; ask for the help of the Holy Spirit to live out your plan. Call upon your guardian angel, a saint, and our Blessed Mother to pray for you!

Appendix C

Nine Essentials of a Disciple Maker

A Guide for Self-Reflection and Discussion

1. Feed your own connection to Christ.

> *"I am the vine, you are the branches. . . . Apart from me*
> *you can do nothing."*
> —John 15:5

- How is your prayer life going?

- What does God seem to be teaching you right now?

- In what part of the Discipleship Wheel are you struggling or growing the most right now?

- Name one hope or goal you have right now for growing in your connection to Christ. What is your plan for reaching it? Potential setbacks? Progress?

2. Commit to others' connection to Christ.

We have a role to play in helping others grow as disciples.

- Whom are you called to guide/accompany in following Jesus?

- What does this involve right now for each person on your list? What do they need? How can you help?

3. Be an intercessor.

Prayer is powerful even when effects aren't visible. We intercede for others because we believe this and want to act in Christian service and love. That is every Christian's call.

- How faithfully and in what ways are you praying for the people you know?

- What is your way of remembering details from people's lives and their prayer requests and ensuring that you follow through on praying for them (a notebook, journal, mobile prayer app, calendar reminder, etc.)?

4. Prayerfully prepare.

Love requires prayerful reflection, thinking ahead, and intentional focus.

- Do you review your notes faithfully and seek the Holy Spirit's lead to prepare your one-on-one meetings? (This need not be a lengthy process, but you should devote at least some intentional time to prayerful preparation.)

- What approaches and/or content are you using in your one-on-ones? How well are these suited to each person?

5. Get to know the person.

Without genuine understanding and care, all attempts to serve fall flat.

- What motivates this person? What hopes and desires have they shared with you?

- What victories or joys have they recently experienced?

- What obstacles are they facing? Which of these do they recognize?

6. Be trustworthy.

"He who is faithful in a very little is faithful also in much."
—Luke 16:10

- Have you maintained the confidentiality that this person deserves?

- Have you followed through on everything you promised?

- Do you avoid dragging people into unnecessarily complex or confusing considerations?

- When the opportunities have arisen, have you done your best to present Church teaching in a positive and charitable light?

7. Share your life.

We were ready to share with you not only the gospel of God but also our own selves, because you had become very dear to us
—1 Thessalonians 2:8

- Do you ever do things outside of getting together to talk about discipleship?

- Do you share details from your own life and ask for their prayers?

8. Be patient.

Love is patient and kind.
—1 Corinthians 13:4

- Have you let your "agenda" run ahead of what this person needs right now?

- How is your attempt to accompany this person stretching or challenging you?

9. Get over yourself!

He must increase, but I must decrease.
—John 3:30

- What fears or worries must you renounce in order to accompany this person?

- Are you called to help them connect with any other individuals or groups?

Appendix D

Tips for Motivating Change

You can find many books by Christians and others on how people change. No single answer exists, but your goal in one-on-ones must be to seek how God is leading you to help people grow from one stage of spiritual maturity to the next. You can do this through lovingly gentle guidance and assisting people to hear the prompts of the Holy Spirit. The suggestions below won't work without your love and acceptance of the people you're mentoring, but they can help you to help them change.

When people seem stuck and unable to make positive changes, we can get frustrated and discouraged. That can cause us to resort to tactics that may be too heavy-handed. When that happens, the people we want to help can become discouraged or feel badgered: a sure recipe for losing them.

Of course, prayer remains all-important because only the Holy Spirit can bring conviction and desire for growth in holiness. In addition to prayer, below are a few tips and considerations for helping the Spirit to motivate someone gently and effectively:

Encourage People to Set Helpful Goals or Actions

"If you aim at nothing, you'll hit it every time."[67]

Articulating goals or a next step/action is an indispensable practice for achieving positive change. You need not be a motivational speaker or a professional life coach to help a friend identify and articulate ways they want to change. Once they share a hope or a goal with you, it makes your role in the one-on-one much clearer and easier. You remind, support, encourage, and assist them in accomplishing their goal. You share some of your own goals with them as well. This holds you accountable, improves your witness, and strengthens your friendship.

There is no shortage of wisdom around us on goal setting. One of the simplest and most universally acknowledged tips for success is to set SMART goals.

SMART goals are Specific, Measurable, Achievable, Relevant and Time Bound. "I want to pray more" is not specific, measurable, or time bound. "I will pray for an hour every morning before my kids wake up" is probably not achievable or relevant to the life of a parent of young children.

A few examples of SMART goals:

- **"I will pray for fifteen minutes a day using the Gospel of the day for three weeks."**

- **"I will go to Mass one more day a week than I currently go, for one month."**

Help those whom the Lord has put in your life to identify, write down, and follow through on their goals to grow in following Jesus. Remind them to set small goals, to expect to struggle, and to adjust their plan as needed. It's a marathon, not a sprint! And help them never to forget that God's love and mercy are not dependent upon their performance. Use the Discipleship Wheel (appendix A), Discipleship Plan (appendix B), and the rest of the *Nextstep* content (in print and online) to help people identify their next steps.

A Five-Step Framework to Motivating Change

The following framework presumes a relationship of mutual trust and friendship, like you would have in a regular one-on-one after some time.

1. Prompt them to articulate a goal or step. Ask them to articulate one way that they would like to take a step forward in their life with Christ.

2. Ask them to identify obstacles to accomplishing this goal. This probably isn't the first time they are thinking about this goal. Why haven't they accomplished it yet? What's holding them back? Is it a scheduling issue, a lack of clarity, a fear or temptation, etc.? Without a plan to address it, whatever stood in their way in the past is likely to do so this time as well.

3. Help them create a realistic plan: how can they reach this goal in a specific, achievable way? Help them adjust their goal to be SMART (Specific, Measurable, Achievable, Relevant, and Time Bound). You might not use the actual term "SMART goal," but rather, ask a few questions to help them make any vague hopes more concrete and manageable. Encourage them to set short-term benchmarks; many people need to experience "quick wins" to stay motivated, at least at first. Don't let their goals be too lofty, or you'll both get discouraged. Faithfulness to small steps builds momentum towards larger strides.

4. Ask how you can help them. What support or accountability do they desire? Perhaps a text message or a call at a certain time? Perhaps to accomplish part of the goal together sometime soon? Do they need more information or to connect with someone else?

5. Always be generous in affirmation, encouragement, and prayer for this person.

Don't try to do these steps at each and every meeting. Just bear them in mind as you're considering the overall progress of your one-on-ones. Most people will need to adjust their goals and strategies many times as they undergo trial and error. It's all part of the process. Mentoring another in discipleship isn't about mastering all the details of the journey; it's about journeying together. Don't be the noisome traveling companion thumping the itinerary. Enjoy the journey and help them enjoy it too!

Three Styles of Guidance

These guidance techniques may be helpful for motivating people in gentle but effective ways. Different people will need different approaches, and you have your own strengths and styles. Before trying any, pray about which technique could utilize your strengths and meet the needs of your one-on-one partner.

Directive Guidance

- Direct them or suggest to them what to do.

- Examples: "You might want to try . . ." "Why don't you . . ." "You could . . ." "I really want to encourage you to . . ." (In general, avoid "should"—most people sufficiently beat themselves up with "should" without any help from others.)

- This works well for people who are both teachable and driven, and who want to be challenged (think soldier/athlete types).

- This could work well for you if you're a natural motivator (coach, teacher, etc.).

Facilitative Guidance

- Facilitate them to come to their own conclusions.

- Examples: "What do you think the Lord wants you to do about that?" "What do you think are the obstacles standing in your way?" "What do you think would be a reasonable goal?"

- Use this with people who are less teachable and more self-motivating and are verbal processors.

- This is a promising approach for discipleship mentors who are good listeners and teachers, detail oriented, less assertive, and/or do not have a charism for inspiring/exhorting.

Collaborative Guidance

- Examples: "Would you want to read this together?" "Let's do this together!" "How can I walk with you in this?" "Would you mind if I did that with you?"

- You must actually follow through and do what you offer.

- Extroverts and sanguine personalities respond well to this, as do people who have short attention spans or lack order and discipline. Use collaborative guidance for anyone who may need extra hand-holding, who may be timid, new to the spiritual life, or doubting.

- People best suited for this need the time to do it and a strong desire to journey closely with others. It's an easy way to get to know the person even better if the relationship seems stuck at too shallow a level.

Desire + Discipline = Delight

A final tip comes by way of an equation that rings true of human experience. Learning to **delight** in something new requires both a **desire** to change and the **discipline** to practice. Think of learning to play an instrument. In order to enjoy playing the piano, we must have both a desire to play well and the discipline to practice even when we do not yet have the skills that make it enjoyable.

If we lack either desire or discipline, we will not get to delight, but to other "d" words. If we only desire something, but lack discipline to practice, we're just dreaming, and our goal never becomes reality. If we force ourselves through the disciplines but lack desire to achieve the end goal, we experience not delight but drudgery. Anyone whose parents made them take piano lessons for too long when they had no desire to be a pianist knows this kind of drudgery well!

In guiding and supporting a growing disciple, we must observe the level of the person's desire for specific spiritual goals and disciplines. Our own enthusiasm can make us assume others share our desire, and we can too quickly encourage a practice with someone who doesn't share our interest.

For someone who wants with all their heart to pray, tips on dealing with distractions or scheduling prayer times inspire and motivate. But for the person lacking any desire to pray more, tips on the discipline of prayer are the last thing they need. We can better serve such people by pondering together the value of prayer or helping them to voice their doubts about it or exposing them to some Scriptural promises or compelling testimonies. These build up desire that make people want the discipline.

By contrast, if someone speaks beautifully about their high desires and hopes for growing in prayer but never seems to make any progress in practice, then they may want you to challenge and encourage them by offering relevant disciplines, tips, and strategies.

For various tips that may help with both desire and discipline for daily prayer, see additional *Nextstep* content online at www.ecnextstep.com. Remember also, your own experience provides your most valuable source of "content." Share your struggles and how you have learned to navigate them, as well as the rewards of disciplines you have developed.

Nature and Grace

For spiritual work, always remember the primacy of grace. As helpful as these strategies may be, we can misunderstand and misuse them all if we lose sight of God and lean exclusively on our planning and efforts.

Catholic Tradition insists that grace builds upon nature. Grace does not destroy, eliminate, or work completely apart from nature: human reason and effort remain relevant and immensely important. If we neglect what we can control (like setting goals, going to bed and waking up on time, showing up for prayer, etc.), we cannot expect God's grace to save the day and override our indolence.

The success of our natural efforts does, however, depend completely on grace. God's grace exceeds and expands nature in ways far beyond our control and gifts. God provides healing, mercy, help, and virtue as free gifts, according to his will and timing. The Holy Spirit convicts us about what must change in our interior and exterior lives. Jesus comforts us with his love by being with us even unto the end of time. All these supernatural blessings beget change in others as techniques and strategies never could.

Our lives display a powerful and mysterious mix of divine action and human cooperation. This definition of a spiritual discipline (also called a practice) succinctly summarizes this interplay of grace and our efforts.

A spiritual discipline is an action or exercise that we can choose to do in order to receive from God the ability (or power) to do what we cannot do by direct human effort alone.[68]

Left to our own devices, we do not have the strength to avoid sin, love enemies, turn away from lustful passions, live generously, or display any of the thousands of ways to imitate Christ. Yet with God's grace, these things become possible. As the spiritual disciplines open us and allow the Holy Spirit to carve out new space within us, we become able to receive the grace God longs to give us.

When setting goals and helping people grow in grace, we focus on spiritual disciplines because these are what humans can do to open ourselves to receive what only God can give. (Spiritual disciplines include praying daily in various ways, receiving the sacraments, serving others concretely, etc.)

We cannot attain spiritual goals on our own. We might want to be less angry, but just wanting it doesn't make it happen. We can choose, however, the spiritual discipline of writing down each day three things for which we are grateful and thanking God for them. That achievable, measurable goal is within our control.

Let's do what we can, so that God can do what we can't— in us.

Appendix E

Questions of the Heart:
A Primer for Deepening our Spiritual
Growth and Conversations

"What are you looking for?"
—John 1:38, NRSV

What Questions Are We Asking?

We can learn a lot about ourselves by directing our attention to the questions we are asking. Whether we're conscious of it or not, we're always asking questions—from the mundane (What should I wear today?) to the profound (What is the purpose of my life?). To be human is to seek, to quest, to ask, and to answer lots and lots of questions.

The questions we ask determine much of what we will find. We rarely find answers to questions we aren't asking.

So what are you looking for? These are the first words of Jesus in John's Gospel. Jesus seemed particularly intent on getting people to ask the right questions, or at least better questions. His questions are powerful, unnerving at times, and transformative for the person who takes them seriously. Jesus gets right to the *heart of the matter*, which is so often the human heart itself, "for the LORD sees not as man sees; man looks on the outward appearance, but the LORD looks on the heart" (1 Samuel 16:7).

The Mind and the Heart

The heart is the source from which our words and actions flow (see Luke 6:43-45). It is the biblical way of referring to the center of our being. Call it the soul, the true self, our character, or any other word that indicates our deepest identity.

While the mind seeks to gain information and put it to some use, the heart seeks to truly "know"—in the rich, biblical sense of the word, which goes far beyond "head knowledge." It is an intimate, relational kind of knowledge, the kind shared between persons. It means to experience, to embrace with one's whole self, to respond fully and live out the implications of the truth or relationship. In a word, to *know* means to *love*.

When Jesus says, "You will know the truth, and the truth will make you free" (John 8:32), he is not speaking of merely agreeing with some godly information. Nor is he speaking only of *believing* in God, for "even the demons believe" (James 2:19). His ultimate prayer is "that they know thee the only true God, and Jesus Christ whom thou hast sent" (John 17:3). The truth that sets us free is Jesus himself—sought and embraced deeply in the human heart.

Every time we encounter the love of God or grow in knowledge (love) of God, something inside of us strengthens. From there it can spill forth into loving words, actions, and the ongoing transformation of our world.

Let us pay close attention, then, to the questions our hearts are asking and to the questions Jesus wants our hearts to ask. They are the doorways through which we enter further into the freedom Jesus bestows.

Introduction to Fifty Questions of the Heart

Below is a list of fifty sample "questions of the heart" that we disciples of Jesus may find ourselves asking and answering in many ways.

We ask and answer questions like these in prayer, in study, and with the help of a few trusted companions. We ask them of Jesus, and we draw upon the riches of Catholic Tradition to help us in asking and answering them over the course of our lives. Whether the answers come quickly or over many years, whether they come only partially or never at all on this side of heaven, perhaps these questions paint something of a portrait of the seeking heart of a Catholic disciple.

Three Ways to Use This List

1. Cultivate your own seeking heart.

First, use this list to help you examine what "questions of the heart" you are currently asking yourself and God. Maybe some on this list will become (or have already been) part of your quest. Maybe there are others, not contained on this list, that your heart is asking. Maybe you have been avoiding your heart, staying at the surface of things. In this case, prayerfully reviewing this list could help you reestablish a connection with your heart and with God who dwells there.

After reading through the list once, go back over it slowly and prayerfully. Don't attempt to answer the questions right away. Rather, over the course of a few prayer times, try to identify *which* two to four questions your heart is drawn to ask right now. Or, after reading the list of questions, write one or more of your own. The list is just an aid to make more explicit the quest of your own heart.

Once you have identified a few questions your heart most wants to ask right now, begin devoting some regular prayer times to asking them. Invite God to help you ask and answer these questions. Draw upon Catholic wisdom and practices to help you. Put no time constraints upon receiving answers. Just bring your questing heart to God.

Journal your questions and thoughts. If you have some faint impressions what some answers might be, journal those too. Make this kind of asking, pondering, and journaling part of your regular prayer life. Let the awareness of your questions become a new lens for your spiritual life. Sometimes we try to size up our spiritual health merely by examining our spiritual practices and daily actions. We must also learn to identify the questions of our hearts and bring them to God.

2. Seek companionship or guidance from another.

As you identify your heart's questions and bring them to the Lord, share some of your quest with another Christian of similar or more advanced spiritual maturity. This can be a spiritual director or a friend who takes the pursuit of God at least as seriously as you do.

You are not expecting answers from this person, just companionship and support in the quest. If you meet with a spiritual director, your director will know how to support you. If you meet with a friend, compare notes with one another in each of your quests, discuss, and pray for one another.

We were not made to live this adventure of discipleship alone. Yet for too many of us, our growth is stunted simply because we don't talk about our spiritual lives with other Christians.

3. Lead deeper conversations.

Knowing the terrain of your own heart more clearly, you can better assist others in asking and answering their questions of the heart. Jesus called us to "make disciples" (Matthew 28:19); this involves guiding and assisting others in asking and answering good questions.

Asking others questions of the heart ought never to be something forced or awkward. We must win the right to ask some of these questions through loyal friendship and loving service, and we must be docile to the Holy Spirit who helps us notice and seize the right opportunities. Timing matters greatly.

Navigating discussions around such questions requires that we draw upon a solid formation in Catholic doctrine and spirituality, as well as a rich experiential knowledge of our own journey. However, we need not have theology degrees or certifications in spiritual direction to discuss discipleship with a few people God has placed in our lives. It's not about knowing all things Catholic, but about prompting more journeys of mutual discovery as we walk with others. Once we get the chance to aid someone in their quest, we do so with great reverence, always staying within the riches of the Church's wisdom and guidance.

There are two ways you can use this list to go about deepening conversation towards matters of the heart.

1. Ask some questions of the heart in natural conversations.

Friends care for and accompany one another in the matters of the heart. You might already have some relationships in which you can ask more of these types of questions in order to deepen conversation. Often the most appropriate way to enter the terrain of the heart is to ask follow-up questions when someone lets you in on something in their lives. You can say things like

- **"Tell me more about that."**

- **"How did you get through that?"**

- **"Where is God for you in this?"**

Follow-up questions are in many ways more important for conversation than initial questions. It is good and natural for conversations to start out at a fairly surface level. The key is to find a thread and follow it deeper, without prying or over-stepping bounds of trust and comfort. The more trust builds between people, the more they can ask each other probing questions without appearing judgmental or interrogating.

2. Give this list (or part of it) to a friend to aid future discussions.

This will not be the most natural or common approach, but if you already meet regularly with someone for spiritual con-versation, taking this direct approach could be a fun and easy way to deepen your time together. You could testify to your experience of praying with this list as you invite them to do the same—and then share the journey. Ask them to spend a few days slowly going over the essay above and the list below, identifying three to five questions they are most willing to pray about and discuss with you. Then get together and talk!

There is no one formula for all spiritual conversations. So much depends upon timing, the unique personalities or life experiences of the people involved, and the strength of the relationship. Yet one way or another, missionary disciples find ways to discuss questions of the heart with others. "Making disciples" has as much to do with the questions we ask and with winning the right to ask them as with any teaching or modeling we might hope to do.

Fifty Questions of the Heart

Think about these things.
—Philippians 4:8

The questions below vary from broad to specific and from past to present. Many overlap with one another. They are arranged into two categories: questions of Jesus and the Discipleship Wheel.

Questions of Jesus[69]

These are a sampling of some of the powerful questions Jesus asked.

- "What are you looking for?" (John 1:38, NRSV)

- "What do you want?" (Matthew 20:21)

- "Who do you say that I am?" (Matthew 16:15)

- "What do you want me to do for you?" (Mark 10:51)

- "Do you believe that I am able to [heal you]?" (Matthew 9:28)

- "Why are you afraid?" (Matthew 8:26)

- "Do you not remember?" (Mark 8:18)

- "Do you know what I have done to you?" (John 13:12)

The Discipleship Wheel[70]

This outlines the Church's basic categories for a holistic life in Christ.

Christ the Center

- Jesus called his followers friends, even while he remained their master, teacher, and Lord. What does this mean to you? In what ways do you experience Jesus as a friend? In what ways do you struggle to understand or experience his friendship?

- Where/how are you currently experiencing some of the abundant life (see John 10:10) of Christ in your ordinary life?

- What blessings from God are you savoring right now—or might you savor more of? What does it mean or look like for you to savor a blessing?

- Where/how are you being stretched or challenged (think of situations at work, health issues, family matters, etc.)? Where is God in this for you?

- What do you feel the Lord asking you to trust him with right now?

- What decisions are you currently discerning or praying about? Or what upcoming decisions do you desire to bring before the Lord?

- What negative emotions or thoughts do you find bubbling up from within yourself more often these days (fear, anger, resentment, jealousy, lust, etc.)?

- How do you respond to them?

- Where is God in this for you?

- How might you use this awareness as an opportunity to draw closer to Christ in asking for help and greater awareness?

- Is there a particular lie that you feel the enemy is using to get under your skin and disturb your peace?

- If so, why do you think he chooses that specific lie?

- Is there a wound associated with that lie? Are there some ways you've been hurt that have made you more susceptible to believing this lie?

- Do you feel like you truly believe in the depths of your heart that you are a child of God, and deeply, personally, and unconditionally loved? Why or why not? (It's common for our hearts to doubt this, even while our minds may readily affirm it.)

Prayer

- In this current season of life, what does your prayer life look like? What do you want it to look like? Is there a gap between your desires and your present reality?

- What Person of the Trinity do you find yourself praying to most often? Why do you think that is? What Person of the Trinity feels the least relatable?

- What joys or challenges have you experienced in prayer recently?

- Do you currently have a habit of a regular, daily prayer time? If so, what does that look like? Do you desire to grow in this or to make some change?

- When we pause to pray, prayer can involve talking, listening, and simply being in God's presence. Which of these is easiest for you? Which is most difficult?

- What role does Mary play in your prayer life? Have you ever had any personal experiences of her protection or intercession?

Scripture

- What role does Scripture currently play in your prayer life? What role do you want it to play?

- Did God draw any Scripture passages to your attention recently?

- Are there any Scripture passages that you think of often to give you peace, perspective, or strength? Do you want to search for more passages to use in this way?

- What Scripture passage or story from Jesus' life best depicts what's going on in your life right now?

Sacraments

- What are your most memorable experiences of the sacraments?

- Did God use any of your encounters with the sacraments recently to bless you or encourage you in any way?

- Are there any practices, prayers, or routines that help you approach or receive the sacraments attentively and fruitfully? If not, is this something you would like to explore?

- What is your experience of Confession? What role does this sacrament play in your life? What role do you want it to play?

Community

- Who has been a source of encouragement in your faith journey? How have they helped form you as a Christian?

- Describe your current support network for life and faith. Is there a gap between your present reality and your desires?

- Who is currently drawing strength from you in their Christian faith? How are you called to support them and pray for them?

Evangelization ("Good-News-Ization")

- What does the call of the laity for "spreading the kingdom" (Apostolicam Actuositatem, 20) or "perfect[ing] the temporal order" (7) or to "evangelize [good-news-ize] the world" (Evangelii Nuntiandi, 41) look like most concretely for you right now? Is this a question you want to explore further in prayer?

- Who is the Lord putting on your heart and why? Might you initiate more conversations with them?

- With respect to your career or studies, in what ways can you find God in the details of your work? How can you be "good news" to others and to your field through hard work, excellence, virtuous living, punctuality, professionalism, joy, positivity, etc.?

Obedience/Conformity to Christ

- We are all works in progress as we "grow up in every way into him who is the head, into Christ" (Ephesians 4:15). This is a long and slow process of growth that continues through many ups and downs and various seasons in life. While God cares about our careers and various decisions, what is clear from Scripture is that God is most concerned with forming our character into godliness and maturity.

- In what ways have circumstances or uncertainties in your everyday life provided opportunities to shape your character in virtue and make you Christlike?

- What do you want to be most known for by others once you are gone? What might God want you to be most remembered for by others?

- Are you reading or studying anything regarding some aspect of God, discipleship, or living your vocation? If so, what are you learning? How might this new learning help you become more Christlike in some area of your life?

- Is there a specific virtue you want to ask God to help you grow in right now? What are some situations in which you can practice this virtue?

Some Additional Questions for Spouses and Parents

For Spouses

- What are you most grateful for in your spouse? When is the last time you thanked God for them? When is the last time you affirmed and thanked your spouse for this quality?

- In what concrete ways might you show your spouse more love, attentiveness, forgiveness, patience, understanding, vulnerability, appreciation, or intimacy (pick one or choose another quality)?

- What virtue do you most desire to grow in right now to love your spouse well? Is this a regular theme of your prayer life?

- How are you praying for your spouse? Might you develop this habit more specifically and intentionally? If so, how and when?

- What trials or suffering pertaining to your marriage might you bring to Jesus in order to be more unified with him in his sufferings for his bride, the Church?

For Parents

- How well do you know each of your children (their interests and passions, worries, strengths, etc.)?

- What virtues do you need right now for loving your children well and establishing or maintaining a relationship of communication and trust? How might this become a regular theme of your prayer life?

- How are you praying for your children by name? Might you develop this habit more specifically and intentionally? If so, how and when?

- What trials or suffering pertaining to your children might you bring to God so that you might grow more unified with him in his longing for the safety and well-being of his children?

Notes

1. Francis de Sales, *Introduction to the Devout Life*, trans. and ed. John K. Ryan (New York, NY: Doubleday Image Books, 2003), 200.
2. *Introduction to the Devout Life*, 200.
3. *Introduction to the Devout Life*, 202.
4. Teresa of Avila, *The Collected Works of St. Teresa of Avila, Volume 2,* trans. Kieran Kavanaugh, OCD, and Otilio Rodriguez, OCD (Washington, DC: ICS Publications, 1980), 117.
5. Henri J. M. Nouwen, *You Are the Beloved: Daily Meditations for Spiritual Living* (New York, NY: Convergent Book, 2017), 12.
6. *The Collected Works of St. Teresa of Avila*, 96.
7. Peter Kreeft, *Prayer for Beginners* (San Francisco, CA: Ignatius Press, 2000), 31.

8. Footnote to 2 Timothy 3:16 in the *New American Bible, Revised Edition.*

9. Bishop Robert Barron, transcript of YouTube video, Bishop Barron on Bill Maher's "Religulous," accessed on October 17, 2017, at https://www.youtube.com/watch?v=Sk0el9nH6Q4&t=108s.

10. *Catechism of the Catholic Church,* Second Edition (Washington, DC: United States Conference of Catholic Bishops, 2016), 109, cf. *Dei Verbum,* 12, section 1.

11. *Catechism,* 112, cf. Luke 24:25-27, 44-46; 113, Origen, Homily in Leviticus 5, 5: *Patrologia Graeca* 12, 454D; 114, cf. Romans 12:6.

12. *Catechism* 116, cf. St. Thomas Aquinas, *Summa Theologica,* I, 1, 10, *ad* 1..

13. *Catechism,* 117, cf. 1 Corinthians, 10:2.

14. *Catechism,* 129, cf. St. Augustine, Quaest. in *Hept.* 2, 73: *Patrologia Latina* 34, 623; cf. *Dei Verbum,* 16..

15. *Catechism,* 117, cf. 1 Corinthians 10:11; Hebrews 3-4:11.

16. *Catechism,* 117, cf. Revelation 21:1-22:5.

17. Benedict XVI, Inaugural Session of the Fifth General Conference of the Bishops of Latin America and the Caribbean, Aparecida, May 13, 2007, 3, http://www.vatican.va/content/benedict-xvi/en/speeches/2007/may/documents/hf_ben-xvi_spe_20070513_conference-aparecida.html.

18. see 1 Corinthians 8:1-11; 11:2-16; 17-34.

19. 1 Corinthians 11:21-22, 33-34, NRSVCE.

20. John 13:34; 15:12, 17; Romans 13:8; 1 Thessalonians 3:12; 4:9; 1 Peter 1:22; 1 John 3:11; 4:7, 11; 2 John 5.

21. Fyodor Dostoyevsky, *The Brothers Karamazov* (New York, NY: Farrar, Straus and Giroux, 2002), 55.

22. "[Jesus'] purpose also was that they might accomplish the work of salvation which they had proclaimed, by means of sacrifice and sacraments, around which the entire liturgical life revolves. . . . To accomplish so great a work, Christ is always present in His Church, especially in her liturgical celebrations" (Vatican II, *Sacrosanctum Concilium*, 6, 7), http://www.vatican.va/archive/hist_councils/ii_vatican_council/documents/vat-ii_const_19631204_sacrosanctum-concilium_en.html).

23. *Catechism,* 1116, emphasis added; cf. Luke 5:17; 6:19; 8:46; see also 1127, cf. Council of Trent (1547): Denzinger-Schönmetzer (1965).

24. See John 3:16; Matthew 3:17; Matthew 17:5.

25. *Catechism,* 521, quoting St. John Eudes; Liturgy of the Hours, Week 33, Friday; Office of Readings.

26. *Catechism,* 521.

27. *Catechism,* 1534

28. *Catechism,* 1604

29. *Catechism,* 1547.

30. *Catechism,* 1604.

31. Cardinal Joseph Bernadin, *The Gift of Peace: Personal Reflections,* quoted in *United States Catholic Catechism for Adults*, 250.

32. *Catechism,* 1505.

33. *United States Catechism for Adults*, 254.

34. Mark E. Thibodeaux, SJ, *Reimagining the Ignatian Examen: Fresh Ways to Pray from Your Day* (Chicago, IL: Loyola Press, 2015).

35. Pope St. Paul VI, *Evangelii Nuntiandi*, 14, December 8, 1975, 14, http://www.vatican.va/content/paul-vi/en/apost_exhortations/documents/hf_p-vi_exh_19751208_evangelii-nuntiandi.html.

36. Congregation for the Doctrine of the Faith, *Doctrinal Note on Some Aspects of Evangelization*, 2, http://www.vatican.va/roman_curia/congregations/cfaith/documents/rc_con_cfaith_doc_20071203_nota-evangelizzazione_en.html.

37. Pope St. Paul VI, *Evangelii Nuntiandi*, 14.

38. Congregation for the Doctrine of the Faith, *Doctrinal Note on Some Aspects of Evangelization*, 2.

39. Pope St. Paul VI, *Evangelii Nuntiandi*, 15.

40. Congregation for the Doctrine of the Faith, *Doctrinal Note on Some Aspects of Evangelization*, 2.

41. Pope St. Paul VI, *Evangelii Nuntiandi*, 14.

42. Congregation for the Doctrine of the Faith, *Doctrinal Note on Some Aspects of Evangelization*, 2.

43. Pope St. Paul VI, *Apostolicam Actuositatem* [Decree on the Apostolate of the Laity], 2, November 18, 1965, 2, http://www.vatican.va/archive/hist_councils/ii_vatican_council/documents/vat-ii_decree_19651118_apostolicam-actuositatem_en.html.

44. Pope St. John Paul II, *Christifideles Laici*, 28 [The Lay Members of Christ's Faithful People], December 30, 1988, 28, http://www.vatican.va/content/john-paul-ii/en/apost_exhortations/documents/hf_jp-ii_exh_30121988_christifideles-laici.html.

45. Michael Sean Winters, "The Wrong Meme in Chicago," *The National Reporter*, September 24, 2014.

46. Mother Teresa, *Where There is Love, There is God: Her Path to Closer Union with God and Greater Love for Others* (New York, NY: Doubleday, 2010), 190-91.

47. Pope St. Paul VI, *Evangelii Nuntiandi*, 22.

48. *Evangelii Nuntiandi*, 41.

49. United States Council of Catholic Bishops (USCCB), "Go and Make Disciples: A National Plan and Strategy for Catholic Evangelization in the United States," Introduction, 6-7, http://www.usccb.org/beliefs-and-teachings/how-we-teach/evangelization/go-and-make-disciples/introduction_go_and_make_disciples.cfm..

50. Pope Benedict XVI, *Deus Caritas Est* [God Is Love], December 25, 2005, 1, http://www.vatican.va/content/benedict-xvi/en/encyclicals/documents/hf_ben-xvi_enc_20051225_deus-caritas-est.html..

51. *Deus Caritas Est*, 1.

52. The distinctions and terms used in this module were first articulated by Don Everts and Doug Schaupp in the book *I Once Was Lost: What Postmodern Skeptics Taught Us about Their Path to Jesus.* The stages were appropriated for a Catholic audience by Sherry Weddell in *Forming Intentional Disciples: The Path to Knowing and Following Jesus.* We recommend both these books for a deeper understanding of the stages and strategies for helping people over each threshold.

53. Don Everts and Doug Schaupp, *I Once Was Lost: What Postmodern Skeptics Taught Us about Their Path to Jesus* (Downers Grove, IL: InterVarsity Press, 2008), 32.

54. *I Once was Lost*, 86.

55. *General Directory for Catechesis*, 56b, http://www.vatican.va/roman_curia/congregations/cclergy/documents/rc_con_ccatheduc_doc_17041998_directory-for-catechesis_en.html, quoting *Ad Gentes*, December 7, 1965, 13b.

56. *General Directory for Catechesis*, 67–68.

57. *General Directory for Catechesis*, 50

58. *General Directory for Catechesis*, 70

59. *General Directory for Catechesis*, 58

60. General Directory for Catechesis, 63

61. "Disciples Called to Witness: The New Evangelization," USCCB Committee on Evangelization and Catechesis.

62. *General Directory for Catechesis*, 64.

63. Pope St. Paul VI, *Evangelii Nuntiandi*, 75.

64. Peter Kreeft, *Prayer For Beginners* (Ignatius Press: San Francisco, 2000), 29-30.

65. Adapted by the Evangelical Catholic from Rich Cleveland, *The Catholic Topical Memory System*, "The Wheel Illustration" (Albuquerque, NM: Emmaus Journey, 2006) 17.

66. *The Collected Works of St. Teresa of Avila*, Volume 1, 96.

67. Zig Ziglar, commonly quoted, as in Dave Ramsey, *Dave Ramsey's Complete Guide to Money* (Brentwood, TN: Lampo Press, 2011), 54.

68. *The Life with God Bible: New Revised Standard Version with the Deuterocanonical Books*; ed. Richard J. Foster (New York, NY: HarperCollins Publisher, 2005).

69. Even without careful study of the biblical/historical context in which these questions were asked, we can gain much from asking them of ourselves in prayer. Reading their context in Scripture can lead to even richer meditation.

70. The Discipleship Wheel is congruous with the "Tasks of Catechesis" found in *General Directory for Catechesis*, 84-87, and in the *National Directory for Catechesis*, 20. See appendix A in this volume, and *Nextstep, Volume 1*, chapter 7 for more on the Discipleship Wheel.

About the Authors

Andrea Jackson studied English Language and Literature as an undergraduate at Harvard University and earned a Master's degree of Divinity from the Boston College School of Theology and Ministry. She started intentionally following Jesus as a sophomore in college when another student showed her which next steps to take in her life of discipleship. Andrea worked as a pastoral associate at a parish in the Archdiocese of Boston for four years before joining the team of The Evangelical Catholic as a writer and ministry consultant in 2018. She lives with her husband in Milwaukee, Wisconsin.

Andre Lesperance is a senior ministry consultant and writer at The Evangelical Catholic. He has worked in full-time Catholic ministry and education since 2003 and holds a master's degree in theology from Marquette University. In both his personal and professional life, Andre's passion lies in helping others to grow in the riches of life in Christ Jesus by identifying and taking their next steps. He lives with his wife and four children near Milwaukee, Wisconsin.